An Introduction to Parallel Programming

An Introduction to Parallel Programming

K. Mani Chandy
Stephen Taylor

California Institute of Technology
Pasadena, California

JONES AND BARTLETT PUBLISHERS
BOSTON

Editorial, Sales, and Customer Service Offices
Jones and Bartlett Publishers
20 Park Plaza
Boston, MA 02116

Library of Congress Cataloging-in-Publication Data

Chandy, K. Mani.
   An introduction to parallel programming / K. Mani Chandy and Stephen Taylor.
      p. cm.
   Includes index.
   ISBN 0-86720-208-4
   1. Parallel programming (Computer science)   I. Taylor, Stephen.
  1956- . II. Title.
QA76.642.C47 1992
004′.35—dc20   91-29918
ISBN: 0-86720-208-4   CIP

Consulting Editors: J. C. Browne and John S. Werth
                      Computer Science Department
                      University of Texas at Austin

Layout Design and Typesetting: Anna S. Taylor
Cover Design: Hannus Design Associates
Repro Output and TEX/POSTSCRIPT *Programming:* Publishing Experts

Printed in the United States of America
95 94 93 92 91   10 9 8 7 6 5 4 3 2 1

To our Fathers
K.T. Chandy *and* G.F.W. Taylor

Contents

Preface

This book is an introductory parallel programming text. The book describes fundamental methods by which programs are assembled, or *composed*. All of our programs are developed from specifications using three basic composition strategies that signify parallel execution, choosing between alternatives and sequential execution. The ideas in the book are language independent and can be implemented using any convenient programming system; however, the book is also supported by a practical implementation, freely available from Caltech, that operates on a wide range of multicomputers, shared memory machines and networks of workstations.

A book of this type can use formal notations for both specifications and programs, or it can describe these informally in English. There are relative advantages to both options. An informal description allows a simplicity in communication and a focus on the main themes; unfortunately, it tends to be imprecise and prone to error. Formal descriptions allow difficult algorithmic questions to be answered precisely. This book provides a blend of both practical programming techniques and formal theory.

Our goal is to reach students within a wide range of computing and mathematical skills; we are particularly concerned with students who have been exposed to sequential programming but have not encountered parallel programming or perceived the need for formal methods. This goal has led to some decisions concerning the presentation of the material. First, we assume that our readers have had a minimal exposure to the ideas of sequential programming. Second, we have decided to introduce the concepts informally, via programming examples, to develop the readers intuition. Finally, we develop and use formal definitions to make our intuition precise.

Acknowledgments

Caltech. The authors are grateful to the faculty of computer science, in particular, Alain Martin, Chuck Seitz and Jan van de Snepscheut for their encouragement and support while conducting this research. Caltech provides a unique atmosphere in which to carry out research and is one of the few institutions in which parallel computing is taught to undergraduates, even in Freshman and Sophomore years. We are particularly grateful to our students in CS 138 and CS 140 who have made many valuable comments on both the book and PCN software.

Research Funding. The initial seed funding for the work presented in this book was provided by the Defense Advanced Research Projects Agency (DARPA) under order number 6202. The research on compositional design of reactive systems was funded by the Air Force Office of Scientific Research under grant AFOSR-91-0070, and formal methods was funded by the Office of Naval Research under grant N00014-89-J-3201. Many of the ideas in this book were developed over the last three years with funding from the National Science Foundation Center For Research in Parallel Computing (NSF-CRPC), under cooperative agreement CCR-880-9615.

The research that went into this book could not have been carried out without the support of these agencies. We are particularly grateful to Charlie Holland of AFOSR, Nat Macon of NSF, Gary Koob and Andre van Tilborg of ONR, and Gil Weigand of DARPA for their advice.

Colleagues. The central idea in this book is that structured parallel programs can be constructed by composing smaller programs using three compositional operators — sequential, parallel and choice composition; in other words, we can design large parallel programs, with clean structures, by putting smaller programs together in well-defined ways. The notation for designing parallel programs in this way is called Program Composition Notation (PCN), and has been developed jointly by the authors. The theory, notation and implementation of PCN is derived in part from our earlier work on UNITY with Jayadev Misra, and *Strand* with Ian Foster. We are thankful to them for their cooperation.

The PCN implementation effort owes much to the contributions of a number of individuals. Ian Foster has made numerous contributions both to the design and implementation of the tools, especially in the areas of run-time systems and source-to-source compilation. The quality of the PCN programming system is largely due to the efforts of the implementation team, in particular, Steve Tuecke (run-time systems), Sharon Brunett (compiler and testing procedures), Jan Lindheim (source-to-source transformations), Dong Lin (syntax translation), David Long (prototyping environment) and Melody Hancock (user interface). Carl Kesselman has been responsible for the design and implementation of all performance measurement and analysis tools. The authors are very grateful to the PCN team for their efforts and enthusiasm.

Considerable applications development efforts have been made by teams at Caltech, Argonne National Laboratory and The Aerospace Corporation. The example programming projects in Part II of the book were designed and implemented in collaboration with three talented undergraduates: Dong Lin (structured grids), Truxton Fulton (irregular grids) and Robert Lister (N-body simulation); our sincere thanks to all for their thoroughness and enthusiasm. The problems were proposed by Roy Williams and John Salmon of Caltech, who rendered considerable help in understanding and describing the problems; our thanks to both.

The authors are thankful for the support received from their colleagues in CRPC. The authors have greatly benefited from comments and interactions with Berna Massingill, John Thornley and Helmut Rainel. Johan Lukkien and Peter Hofstee listened to talks on the theory of composition, very early in the game, and their criticism was most helpful.

K.M. Chandy taught compositional programming at the NATO Summer School on Programming at Marktoberdorf, Germany, in the summer of 1990, while the ideas were still being conceptualized. The students at the school were constructive in their criticism. The author is particularly thankful to Tony Hoare, one of the directors of the school, for his suggestions.

Book Design. The book was designed and typeset by Anna Taylor. Thanks to her for another marvelous job. Thanks also to David Mallis of Publishing Experts for all his hard work on TEX macros and document preparation.

An Introduction to Parallel Programming

Part I

Basic Concepts

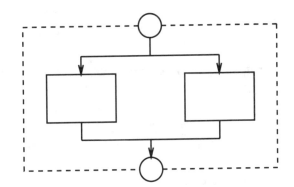

CHAPTER

1

Parallel Programming

In essence, the task of the programmer is:

*Given a specification, develop a program
that satisfies the specification.*

A **parallel program** is simply a collection of cooperating programs that together satisfy a given specification.

In this book, the phrase *parallel program* is used in its broadest sense. It includes the programs that control space vehicles exploring the universe, circuits on a chip, and scientific applications that execute on concurrent supercomputers. It includes concurrent programs, distributed programs, communicating processes, and cooperative systems. It includes programs written in different programming languages and paradigms: C, Fortran, Pascal; object-oriented, functional and logic programs. The book carries a message, and the message is:

All programs have a common theory and design method.

Much of this book is concerned with *transformational* programs: programs that are specified by their initial and final states. We also provide a brief introduction to *reactive* programs: programs that interact with their environment during execution and cannot be specified purely in terms of their initial and final states.

3

1.1 Program Composition

Our goal is to help programmers develop parallel programs methodically by focusing attention on the central concept of **program composition**:

> *The method by which programs are put together*
> *to form larger programs.*

Throughout this book we will build programs using three basic strategies: **parallel, choice** and **sequential** composition. Inevitably, program components must *share* information, and we use **variables** to characterize this sharing. The language in which a particular component is stated is irrelevant; its *meaning* is our concern. By shifting emphasis away from the operation of each statement and toward how programs are assembled, we emphasize methodical design.

To introduce the concept of composition, we have organized the book into three distinct parts: Basic Concepts, Parallel Program Design and Design Theory. The first part contains preliminary ideas and notations that we will use to develop programs. It is intended to gradually, through examples, build the reader's intuition on how to express, understand and reason about programs. Key ideas are emphasised in the text by enclosing them boxes, for example:

Program Composition: There are three basic ways to *compose* programs: in parallel, by choice or sequentially. Program components share information.

The second part of the book extends that of the first to illustrate the design of non-trivial programs. Problems that are particular to parallel programming are discussed and a variety of simple but useful programming techniques are outlined. The goal of this part is to illustrate the main program design methodology: **stepwise refinement**. The essence of good design practice is the incremental, reasoned development of a program from an initial specification. At each step in this refinement process, the main activity is to separate concerns so as to deal with seemingly interrelated problems individually. Parallel program design is no exception to this rule: Programs may be constructed using the same methical process that has been used in the construction of sequential programs. The central difference is that new refinement steps are needed to deal with problems particular to parallel programming.

Finally, in the third part of the book, we formalize the intuitive notions developed in the first two parts. In particular, an **operational semantic** is developed that allows us to describe abstractly the operation of a parallel program on any computer. We also present rules for proving the correctness of programs. These rules form the basis of an **axiomatic semantic**. Using this body of theory it is possible to reason about programs in a mathematically precise manner. It is also possible to incrementally refine the *program specification* and *mechanically translate* the specification into an equivalent program.

1.2   Is Parallel Programming Hard?

The conventional wisdom is that parallel programming is extremely hard, much harder than sequential programming; hence students should get a thorough grounding in sequential programming at the undergraduate level before they are introduced to parallel programming in graduate school. We believe this to be incorrect and that for many practical tasks:

Parallel programming can be easier than sequential programming.

Sequential programming, and its attendant concept of state, are difficult concepts to understand and use; they should be placed within the overall context of the program design process as *refinements* concerned with the economy of space and time.

Programming is considerably simplified if we work in the domain of the problem to be solved — the specification domain — rather than on coding for some particular machine. This belief has led us to teach parallel programming to undergraduates via stepwise refinement of specifications. Indeed, some of our best students are undergraduates with little or no previous programming experience — freshmen and sophomores.

1.3   Notations

Our specifications are expressed in the universal notation of the **predicate calculus**. Our programs are stated in a **Program Composition Notation (PCN)** that can be executed directly on a wide variety of parallel machines; these include networks of workstations, multicomputers and shared-memory multiprocessors. The PCN software is in the public domain and is freely available from Caltech. To obtain the software use anonymous FTP from the *pcn* directory at *sampson.caltech.edu* (131.215.145.136).

The programming notation is very close to the specification notation. Indeed, we think of the programming notation as a restriction of the specification notation, such that the restricted notation is *executable*. An advantage of this similarity between specification and programming notation is that one can think of the programs in this book as specifications: The work of refining a given specification into a composition of simpler specifications has already been carried out. The program can either be executed directly or can be further refined into a language of the programmer's choice. Therefore:

> *The central ideas of this book are language-independent.*

The programming notation is provided to make programs precise, and is intended for readers who want to directly execute their programs on parallel or sequential computers.

1.4 How to Read this Book

Freshmen who have *not* completed a course in discrete mathematics should read the book from the beginning to the end in order. In some early chapters, specifications and corresponding programs may be presented before an explanation is given. We suggest that you stop, consider the program and determine what new concepts are being introduced. The subsequent explanation confirms or corrects your intuition.

Students who have already had a course in discrete mathematics should begin by reading the first three chapters to gain familiarity with our programming notations. The second and final parts of the book should then be studied more carefully. If any programming concepts are unclear in the second part of the book, refer to the first part for clarification.

Students with some degree of mathematical sophistication may focus attention on the final part of the book and skim the rest, focusing on areas of particular interest.

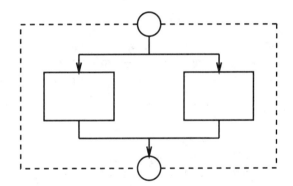

CHAPTER

2

Composing Parallel Programs

> **Goals for this Chapter:**
>
> At the end of this chapter you should understand the concepts of *definition statement, choice composition, parallel composition*, and *recursion*. You should also understand the idea of a *termination condition* and a *metric*.

This chapter introduces two methods for assembling programs: *choice* and *parallel* composition. Program components share information via *definition variables* and execute repeatedly using the concept of *recursion*. The concepts of *termination condition* and *metric* are introduced in order to clarify how programs operate.

2.1 Definition Statements and Boxes

A **definition statement** is a program of the form:

$$variable = value$$

The role of this program is to define, once and for all, the value of the **definition variable** written on the left. Prior to the execution of the statement, the variable has no associated value and is **undefined**; afterward, the variable is equivalent to the value on the right and remains unchanged *forever*. For example, consider the statement:

index = 5

Initially, the variable, named index, is undefined; the definition signifies that the variable is defined to be the value 5, an integer. Any use of the variable in a program is thus equivalent to the use of the value 5.

A definition variable can be regarded as a **box** as shown in Figure 2.1. The box has a label corresponding to the name of the variable and is initially empty. The role of a definition statement is simply to place a value into the box.

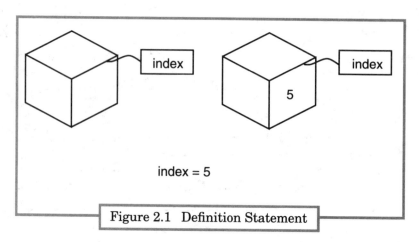

index = 5

Figure 2.1   Definition Statement

2.1.1   What Values Can Be Placed in a Box?

The basic types of information, or data, that we may wish to place inside a box correspond to integers, floating point numbers and character strings. For example, the following are examples of definitions involving these values:

maximum = 23

age = 34

PI = 3.142

Radius = 5.0

$$\text{persons\_name} = \text{``paul''}$$

$$\text{Brick\_Type} = \text{``Lego''}$$

Sometimes it is valuable to be able to place one box inside another or, rather, to define variables to be equivalent. For example,

$$\text{low\_limit} = \text{high\_limit}$$

$$\text{my\_raise} = \text{your\_raise}$$

Another type of value we may wish to place in a box is an **arithmetic expression**. For example,

$$E = M * (C * C)$$

$$\text{area} = \text{PI} * (\text{radius} * \text{radius})$$

$$\text{mean} = (\text{value1} + \text{value2}) / 2$$

$$\text{raise} = \text{old\_salary} + \text{epsilon}$$

Our arithmetic expressions involve variables, numbers and operators such as multiplication ($*$), addition ($+$), subtraction ($-$), division ($/$) and modulus ($\%$).

Finally, it is often useful to collect a number of values together, consider them as a single entity, and place them into a box. We call a collection of items a **tuple** and denote a tuple containing n ($n \geq 0$) values by the notation

$$\{ \text{ value}_0, \text{ value}_1, \ldots, \text{value}_{n-1} \}$$

Typically, the values placed inside a tuple are numbers, strings and variables; however, it is also reasonable to place tuples inside each other. The resulting structure corresponds to a **tree** of information. For example, the definitions

$$\text{tree} = \{ \text{ ``pine''}, \{ 1991, \text{age, height} \}, \text{``yellowstone''} \}$$

$$\text{age} = \{ 66, \text{``years''} \}$$

$$\text{height} = \{ 15, \text{``feet''} \}$$

are equivalent to the single definition

$$\text{tree} = \{ \text{ ``pine''}, \{ 1991, \{ 66, \text{``years''} \}, \{ 15, \text{``feet''} \} \}, \text{``yellowstone''} \}$$

This tree, of depth three, is shown pictorially in Figure 2.2 and demonstrates that tuples may be used to build arbitrary n-ary tree structures.

There is one particular method for organizing data that we use frequently: It represents a *sequence* of values and is termed a **list**. For example, the following definition denotes a list of numbers between one and five inclusive.

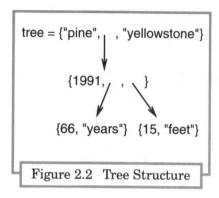

Figure 2.2   Tree Structure

$$mylist = [1,2,3,4,5]$$

A list containing no elements is denoted [ ]. A list can also be denoted as [first | rest]. For example, the following definitions define mylist to be [1,2].

$$mylist = [first \,|\, rest]$$

$$first = 1$$

$$rest = [second \,|\, rest1]$$

$$second = 2$$

$$rest1 = [\,]$$

The elements of a list and arguments of a tuple may be any other data type. Thus the following, not particularly meaningful, definitions are legitimate.

$$mylist = [1,\{[2,\{3,\text{``hello''},4\}],5\},99.9]$$

$$mytree = \{[1,2],[\,],\{\text{``hello''},[3.7]\}\}$$

The central difference between a tuple and a list is that any element of a tuple may be accessed in constant time by indexing, list elements may only be accessed in linear sequence. We will return to this point again in Chapter 3 when describing programs that build and manipulate lists and/or trees.

Definition Variables: Are initially *undefined* and are defined to be equivalent to a value by a definition statement; the value may be a number, string, variable, expression, tuple or list.

Finally, there are some definitions that simply do not make sense. For example, we should not place boxes inside *themselves* or, rather, define variables in terms of themselves. Thus we do not use definitions such as

$$box = box$$

$$box = \{1,box,3\}$$

$$box = \{1,\{2,\{box,3\},4\}\}$$

2.1.2   Why Bother with Boxes?

We will see, as our discussions progress, that boxes, or definition variables, have a number of useful properties. These properties are *not yet apparent* but we briefly outline them here. You should keep the properties in mind in the discussions that follow and try to recognize when they become apparent.

Communication. Imagine you are talking over a telephone with a friend. After you have spoken, the words are gone; you cannot take them back. Your speech carries a *message* that travels from you to your friend and thus some information is *shared* between you.

A definition variable acts just like a message: Initially it is undefined and, once defined, it cannot be changed, or taken back. So a definition statement is an abstraction for *sending a message*, and a tuple is an abstraction for a message containing more than one value. Further, a list corresponds to a *sequence of messages*.

This abstraction for communication is valuable because it is independent of both *language* and *architecture*. The same concept means the same thing, irrespective of the language in which it is expressed or the machine upon which it is implemented. Our conversation may be between workstations connected via a local area network, computers sharing a satellite connection, across a set of wires in a multicomputer or through shared memory in a multiprocessor; it makes no difference.

Synchronization. Imagine, in your telephone conversation, that you and your friend both speak at the same time. The result is confusion. To get around this problem you each *wait* for the appropriate opportunity and then speak, usually at the end of a statement or sentence. This process of waiting until the appropriate time is called *synchronization*.

Definition variables provide a simple way to synchronize. If a variable is undefined, a program *waits* until it is defined and then uses the value.

Program Independence. A consequence of using definition variables for sharing information is that it is possible to understand a program in isolation.

> **Definitions:** Are an abstraction for communication; they provide a simple synchronization method and the ability to understand a program independently.

2.2 Choice Composition

Given a number of alternative programs, *choice composition* provides a method to decide which *one* to execute. Each choice composition has n components, where $n > 0$, called **implications**, and has the form

$$\{ ? \; G_1 \rightarrow C_1, G_2 \rightarrow C_2, \ldots, G_n \rightarrow C_n \}$$

where each G_i ($0 < i \leq n$) is called a **guard** and each C_i is a composition built from one or more programs. A guard provides the ability to make decisions based on arithmetic comparison ($>$, $<$, $>=$, $<=$), equality ($==$), inequality ($!=$) and a variety of other simple testing operations; a complete list of the guard tests used in this book is given in Appendix A.

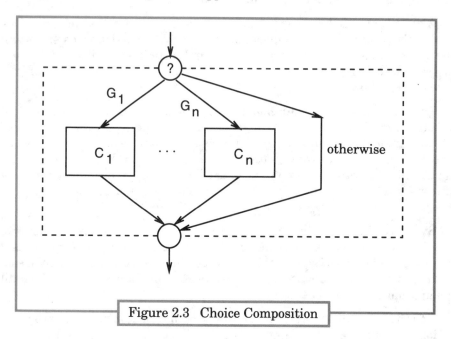

Figure 2.3   Choice Composition

Figure 2.3 shows how a choice composition operates. On entering the composition, if any guard G_i is *true*, then the corresponding implication is chosen and composition C_i is executed. If all guards are *false*, then the entire composition is skipped and does nothing. The choice composition stops executing, or **terminates**, either when C_i terminates or all guards are *false*. For example, consider the following problem specification:

Specification: Write a program minimum(x,y,result) that accepts two numbers x and y; it defines result to be the minimum of these values.

```
minimum(x,y,result)
{ ? x >= y  -> result = y,
    x <= y  -> result = x
}
```

Program 2.1 Minimum of Two Numbers

Program 2.1 implements this specification using choice composition and definition statements. Consider a call to the program: minimum(5,3,result). This call defines the value of x to be 5 and y to be 3. Thus the first guard is *true* and the result is defined to be 3, as expected.

Choice Composition: Selects a *single* composition. If any guard G_i is *true*, then the associated composition C_i is executed. If all guards are *false*, then the composition is skipped. Choice composition terminates when either C_i terminates or all guards are *false*.

Now consider a call minimum(ux,3,result) where the value ux is *not defined* and thus it is not possible to decide if either guard is *true*. The minimum program must *wait* until sufficient information is available to choose between the alternative implications. This forced waiting for information provides a method of program synchronization.

Synchronization: Programs wait until sufficient information is available for guards to be evaluated.

Finally, consider a call to the program of the form minimum(3,3,result). In this case, *both* guards are *true* and we cannot predict which statement will be evaluated: Fortunately, the correct result will still be generated in any event. This inability to decide which statement will be executed is called **nondeterminism** in choice.

Nondeterminism in Choice: If more than one guard is true, we cannot predict which implication is chosen.

Nondeterminism is an essential and important component of parallel programming. It reflects the nature both of computing problems and the underlying parallel machines. Many problems are specified such that *any solution* is sufficient, for example: "find any prime number greater than seven." A program may utilize many computers to solve this problem; each computer generates a possible solution and the first to finish computes the final result. If the program is executed on Tuesday and gives the value 17 and on Wednesday it computes the value 19, both answers are perfectly reasonable. Were we to constrain the program to give the same result, irrespective of the day of the week, we would be *overspecifying the problem*. While this overspecification is simple to achieve, it can be wasteful.

2.3   Parallel Composition

Given some number of programs, *parallel composition* specifies that the programs execute in any order. A parallel composition has the form:

$$\{ ||\ C_1, C_2, \ldots, C_n \}$$

Figure 2.4 shows how the composition operates. All of the component compositions C_i $(0 < i \le n)$ are executed concurrently, and the composition terminates when all of its components terminate.

Nondeterminism in Parallel Composition: Programs composed in parallel execute in any order; we cannot predict the order of execution.

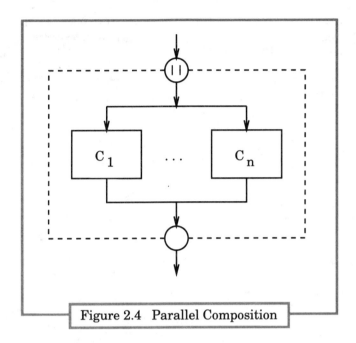

Figure 2.4   Parallel Composition

Consider the following problem specification:

Specification: Write a program min4(a,b,c,d,result) that accepts four numbers, a, b, c and d; it defines result to be the minimum of all four values.

```
min4(a,b,c,d,result)
{||  minimum(a,b,min1),              /* 1 */
     minimum(c,d,min2),              /* 2 */
     minimum(min1,min2,result)       /* 3 */
}
```

Program 2.2 Minimum of Four Numbers

Program 2.2 solves this problem by using three minimum programs that execute concurrently. The solution technique is illustrated in Figure 2.5. In general, when presenting programs we label statements that are particularly important with numbered comments as shown in Program 2.2. In discussing a program, we refer to these statements by mentioning the appropriate statement number in parenthesis, e.g. (1).

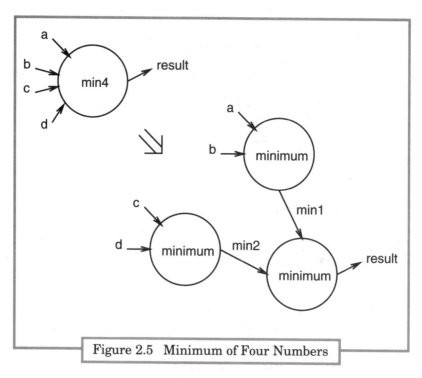

Figure 2.5   Minimum of Four Numbers

To calculate the minimum of all four numbers, the minimum of the first two is calculated to produce a partial result min1 (1). The minimum of the second two numbers is also computed concurrently to form the partial result min2 (2). Finally, the minimum of both partial results, min1 and min2, is computed to obtain the final result (3). Notice how the partial results are *shared* among programs: Information used by more than one program is simply passed to both programs as an argument.

Table 2.1 illustrates how the program executes by detailing one possible execution sequence for the program call min4(9,9,3,26,result). The first column labels each step in the sequence. The second column shows the programs that remain to be executed in a given step. The third column shows which program is picked to execute in the current step and the final column indicates if the program is able to execute or is forced to wait for information.

Initially, there is just a single program to be executed; it is immediately replaced by three programs that execute concurrently. If three computers were available, all three programs might execute at one time. Notice that in steps

Table 2.1: Execution of the min4 Program

Step	Programs	Pick	Result
1	min4(9,9,3,26,result)	←	execute
2	minimum(9,9,min1) minimum(3,26,min2) minimum(min1,min2,result)	←	wait
3	minimum(9,9,min1) minimum(3,26,min2) minimum(min1,min2,result)	←	execute
4	minimum(9,9,min1) min2=3 minimum(min1,min2,result)	←	execute
5	minimum(9,9,min1) minimum(min1,3,result)	←	wait
6	minimum(9,9,min1) minimum(min1,3,result)	←	execute
7	min1=9 minimum(min1,3,result)	←	wait
8	min1=9 minimum(min1,3,result)	←	execute
9	minimum(9,3,result)	←	execute
10	result=3	←	execute
11	**terminate** – result is 3		

2, 5 and 7, a minimum program is unable to execute because its input data is not available. In these cases the program waits and re-occurs in the program list at a subsequent step. In steps 4 and 8 the needed partial results are made available and *communicated* to the remaining minimum program by virtue of definition statements. Thus, eventually, the last program is able to execute and defines the result value to be 3. The entire program terminates when no further programs remain to be executed.

There is one subtle aspect of the program execution that we need to consider further. Consider step 2: What ensures that this program selection is not repeatedly chosen forever preventing program termination? The answer lies in a concept called **fairness**. Our strategy for executing programs obeys the rule that if a program can execute, it will execute *eventually*. We do not specify *when* eventually occurs; it may be seconds or days, depending upon the computer used. This rule ensures that the other programs in our example will terminate, generate partial results and allow the entire program to terminate.

> **Fairness:** A statement that can be executed at any point in an execution is executed eventually.

2.4 Recursion

In all of our programs we will employ just one method for repeatedly executing programs and statements: **recursion**. The essence of this idea is that a program is defined in terms of *itself*. To illustrate the concept, consider the following programming problem:

> **Specification:** Write a program sum(x,y,result) that accepts two positive integers x and y and defines result to be their sum.

```
sum(x,y,result)
{ ? y == 0 -> result=x,                              /* 1 */
    y > 0 ->
        {|| result=1+r1, y1=y-1, sum(x,y1,r1) }      /* 2 */
}
```

Program 2.3 Computing sum with Recursion

Program 2.3 solves this problem by adding one to the value of x, y times. If the value of y is zero, then the result is x (1). Otherwise, the result is 1+r1, where r1 is the sum of x and y-1 (2).

Notice the call to the program sum (shown in boldface) used within the program sum (2). A call of this type is termed a *recursive call*: it calls the program in which it is used. Programs that use calls of this type are called **recursive programs**.

> **Recursive Programs:** Programs that are defined in terms of themselves.

Table 2.2 shows how the program operates given a call sum(5,3,result). In order to distinguish variables associated with a particular recursive call, the variables have been appropriately renamed. Consider each step in the table and be sure you understand how the program operates.

2.4.1 How Do Programs Terminate?

In general, *all* recursive programs must incorporate one or more *conditions* under which they terminate. For example, Program 2.3 provides only one such condition, corresponding to the situation where the value of the argument y is zero (1). There is no recursion associated with the corresponding implication; thus any execution of the program for which y is zero will terminate.

> **Termination Condition:** A condition under which a program stops execution.

2.4.2 How Is Termination Guaranteed?

In general, *all* recursive programs must have some attribute, or measure, of their *progress toward a termination condition*. We call this measure a **metric**. To be sure a program terminates it is necessary to think about how the metric changes.

The metric used in Program 2.3 is the value of the argument y. If y is positive, then the second implication involving recursion is always selected. In every recursive call, the value of y is decremented by one; Table 2.2 highlights the gradual decrease of the value y at steps 1, 3, 5 and 7. Eventually, at step 7, y decreases to the value zero and the first implication is selected. Since this implication does not involve recursion, the program terminates.

> **Metric:** A *measure* that can be used to show that a program is *progressing* toward a point where it will terminate.

Table 2.2: Execution of the min4 Program

Step	Programs	Pick	Result
1	sum(5,3,result)	←	execute
2	result=1+r1 y1=3–1 sum(5,y1,r1)	← ←	wait execute
3	result=1+r1 sum(5,2,r1)	 ←	 execute
4	result=1+r1 r1=1+r2 y2=2–1 sum(5,y2,r2)	← ← ←	wait wait execute
5	result=1+r1 r1=1+r2 sum(5,1,r2)	 ←	 execute
6	result=1+r1 r1=1+r2 r2=1+r3 y3=1–1 sum(5,y3,r3)	 ←	 execute
7	result=1+r1 r1=1+r2 r2=1+r3 sum(5,0,r3)	 ←	 execute
8	result=1+r1 r1=1+r2 r2=1+r3 r3=5	← ← ← ←	wait wait wait execute
9	result=1+r1 r1=1+r2 r2=1+5	← ← ←	wait wait execute
10	result=1+r1 r1=1+6	← ←	wait execute
11	result=1+7	←	execute
12	**terminate** - result is 8		

2.4.3   Alternative Program Formulations

In this section we illustrate two syntactic conveniences that will be used extensively in the programs that follow. Program 2.4 shows an equivalent program
to Program 2.3 that illustrates how to understand arithmetic when used in an
argument position (1). In general, any non-variable argument in a program
call may be replaced by a new variable. The new variable is then defined to
the original argument in parallel with the resulting call. Thus, a call of the
form p(Expression) is equivalent to the composition

$$\{ | | \ \mathsf{new\_variable=Expression, \ p(new\_variable)} \ \}$$

```
        sum(x,y,result)
        { ? y == 0 -> result=x,
            y > 0 ->
                {|| result=1+r1,
                    sum(x,y-1,r1)        /* 1 */
                }
        }
```

Program 2.4 Arithmetic in Arguments

Program 2.5 takes this process one stage further: In this instance, all
arithmetic is performed via argument positions. Since the resulting parallel
composition contains only a *single element*, we may omit the operator and
surrounding braces (1); the same omission may be used for choice composition
when it consists of only a single implication.

```
        sum(x,y,result)
        { ? y == 0 -> result=x,
            y > 0 -> sum(x+1,y-1,result)        /* 1 */
        }
```

Program 2.5 Compositions with a Single Entry

The resulting sum program is somewhat different from previous formulations: the argument x is used as an *accumulator* that gradually progresses
from x to the value x+y. Execute the program by hand and be sure you understand the difference between this program and Program 2.3.

2.5 Summary

In this chapter we have introduced all of the essential ideas that we will use to build parallel programs: Programs are built by *recursive application of parallel and choice composition.* Component programs *communicate* via shared definition variables: Definition statements provide an abstraction for message sending. Program *synchronization* is achieved by testing definition variables: A program waits until sufficient information is available to allow it to continue. Every recursive program must provide *termination conditions* under which it stops execution; a *metric* must exist that makes it possible to verify that a program progresses toward termination.

Exercises

1. Write a tuple that describes yourself.
2. Draw the tree for {1,2,3,X}, {{{1,{2},3},X}}, and {{1,{2},3,X},{1,X}}.
3. Write a *deterministic* minimum program that, when given two inputs, always picks a specific implication.
4. Write a program area(r,a) that computes circle area a using radius r.
5. Write a program bound(b,w,x,y,z,res) that accepts five numbers as input and defines res to be the maximum value among w, x, y and z that is less than bound b.
6. Write a program AND(x,y,z) that accepts two integers x and y; these may be either zero or one. The program defines z to be one if *both* x and y are one; otherwise, z is defined to be zero.
7. Write a program OR(x,y,z) that accepts two strings x and y; these may be either true or false. The program defines z to be true if either x or y is true; otherwise, z is defined to be false.
8. Given the programs

   - zero(x,y) y=0
   - successor(x,y) y=x+1
   - predecessor(x,y) { ? x>0 -> y=x−1, default -> y=0 }

   solve the following problems by composition:

   (a) Write a program product(x,y,z) that accepts two positive integers x and y and defines z to be their product.
   (b) Write a program difference(x,y,z) that accepts two positive integers x and y. The program defines z to be 0 if $x \leq y$; otherwise, z is defined to be x−y.

   Execute your programs by hand and be sure that they operate correctly.

CHAPTER
3

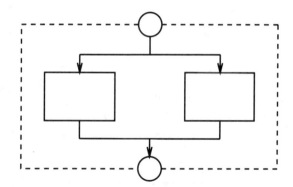

Programming Examples

> **Goals for this Chapter:**
>
> At the end of this chapter you should be able to use the concepts of *definition*, *choice* and *parallel* composition to write concurrent programs. You should also be able to informally check your programs to increase your confidence that they behave correctly and terminate.

In this chapter we solve a variety of simple programming problems to illustrate the use of concepts introduced in Chapter 2. Each problem is first described with an English *specification*. Programs that implement the specification are then given and discussed.

To aid in understanding the programs, we adopt a simple convention: All variables used to denote numbers or strings begin with a lower-case letter; those that denote structured data, such as lists or tuples, begin with a capital letter.

3.1 Simple Arithmetic

In this section we consider two simple recursive programs to help you appreciate recursion. If you do not understand the programs, reread Section 2.4 and execute each program by hand on example inputs.

3.1.1 Power

Specification: Write a program power(x,y,result) that accepts a non-zero integer x and a non-negative integer y. It defines result to be x^y.

```
power(x,y,result)
{ ? y == 0  -> result=1,                              /* 1 */
     y > 0  -> {|| result=x*r1, power(x,y–1,r1) }     /* 2 */
}
```

Program 3.1 Computing power with Recursion

Program 3.1 multiplies x by itself, y times, to form x^y. If y is zero, then x to the power y is 1 (1). Otherwise, the result is x*r1, where r1 is defined to be x to the power y–1. Thus a call power(2,4,result) defines result to be 16.

Recall, from Chapter 2, that every recursive program must have a *termination condition* and a *metric*. In Program 3.1, the termination condition is y==0 and the metric is y. If y is initially positive, every recursive call decreases its value by one; thus the program progresses toward termination.

3.1.2 Factorial

Specification: Write a program factorial(y,result) that accepts a positive integer y and defines result to be y!.

Program 3.2 implements the problem specification. If y is zero, then y! is 1. Otherwise, the result is y*r1, where r1 is (y–1)!. Thus a call factorial(5,result) defines result to be 120.

As in our previous examples, the termination condition is y == 0 and the metric is y. Initially y is positive and every recursive call decreases the value of y by one; thus the program progresses toward termination.

```
factorial(y,result)
{ ? y == 0 –> result=1,                              /* 1 */
    y > 0 –> {|| result=y*r1, factorial(y–1,r1) }    /* 2 */
}
```

Program 3.2 Computing factorial with Recursion

3.2   List Manipulation

Recall that the *list* data structure discussed in Chapter 2 corresponds to a sequence of values. In this section we consider a variety of programs that generate and manipulate these structures.

3.2.1   Generating a List

Specification: Write a program generator(n,L) that accepts a positive integer n and generates a list of integers L in the sequence n,n–1,n–2,...,1.

```
generator(n,L)
{ ? n == 0 –> L = [],              /* 1 */
    n > 0 –>
          {|| L=[n | L1],          /* 2 */
              generator(n–1,L1)    /* 3 */
          }
}
```

Program 3.3 Generating a List

Program 3.3 is a solution to the problem and demonstrates how to construct a list recursively. If n is zero, then the output list is empty (1). If n is greater than zero, then the output list contains n (2) and the rest of the sequence n–1,n–2,...,1; the rest of the sequence is generated by a call to generator with input n–1 (3). Thus, a program call generator(5,Ls) eventually defines Ls to be the list [5,4,3,2,1]. The generator program terminates when the condition n == 0 is satisfied; the metric corresponds to the value n. Initially n is positive. At each recursive call n is decreased by one; thus the program execution progresses toward the termination condition.

3.2.2 Counting Elements

This section introduces a new guard test, **matching**, denoted variable ?= pattern, where pattern is a tuple and may contain numbers, strings, variables, lists, and/or tuples. Matching succeeds if variable is defined and has the form signified by pattern. Tuples match if they are the same size and corresponding arguments match. Lists match if successive elements match. Two numbers or two strings match only if they are identical. A variable in the pattern stands for any element of the structure on the left. To demonstrate the use of matching, consider the following programming problem.

Specification: Write a program count(Ls,cnt) that accepts a list Ls and defines cnt to be the number of elements in Ls.

```
count(Ls,cnt)
{ ? Ls ?= [ ] -> cnt=0,              /* 1 */
     Ls ?= [x | Ls1] ->             /* 2 */
        {|| count(Ls1,cnt1),        /* 3 */
            cnt=cnt1+1              /* 4 */
        }
}
```

Program 3.4 Counting List Elements

Program 3.4 is a naive solution to the problem that demonstrates how to recursively inspect the elements of a list. It uses matching to decompose the structure of the input list Ls. If Ls is empty, then the number of elements it contains is zero (1). Otherwise, the input list comprises two parts corresponding to the first element x and the rest of the list Ls1 (2). The number of elements in the list is the number of elements in the rest of the list (3), plus one (4). Thus, a program call count([19,[],1],cnt) eventually defines cnt to be 3.

The termination condition in Program 3.4 corresponds to the input list Ls being empty. However, unlike our previous examples, there is not an explicit metric. Instead, there is an *implicit* metric that corresponds to the length of the input list. Thus, we restate the termination condition as *the list length is zero*. Notice how the program progresses: Initially, if the list contains some number of elements, then its length is a positive integer. At each recursive call the first element of the list is removed (2). Thus the length of the list decreases by one and gradually approaches zero, the termination condition.

Matching: Used to decompose structures. Two numbers or strings match if they are identical. Tuples match if they are the same size and corresponding arguments match. Lists match if successive elements match. Variables in the pattern stand for an element of the matched structure.

Unfortunately, Program 3.4 is a rather poor program: The value cnt is *not* defined until the expression cnt1+1 is evaluated. This expression cannot be evaluated until the value cnt1 is defined by recursion. Thus the program generates a definition for each element of the input and every definition must wait for subsequent definitions to complete execution.

Program 3.5 is an alternative solution that employs an *accumulator*. Initially the accumulator is zero (1). If the input list is empty, then the result is the accumulator (2). Otherwise, an element is removed from the input and the accumulator is incremented (3). Unlike the naive solution, this program requires no waiting for values to be available. It also illustrates a useful notational convenience: Elements of a matched structure that are not significant are denoted by an anonymous variable "_" (3).

```
count(Ls,cnt) count1(Ls,0,cnt)                     /* 1 */

count1(Ls,acc,cnt)
{ ? Ls ?= [] -> cnt=acc,                           /* 2 */
    Ls ?= [_ | Ls1] -> count1(Ls1,acc+1,cnt)       /* 3 */
}
```

Program 3.5 Counting with an Accumulator

3.2.3 Summing a List

Specification: Write a program sum(Ls,result) that accepts
a list of numbers Ls and defines result to be the sum of the
elements in Ls.

```
    sum(Ls,result) sumlist(Ls,0,result)                /* 1 */

    sumlist(Ls,acc,sum)
    { ? Ls ?= [ ] -> sum=acc,                          /* 2 */
        Ls ?= [x | Ls1]  -> sumlist(Ls1,acc+x,sum)     /* 3 */
    }
```

Program 3.6 Summing a List

Program 3.6 solves this problem using a variation of the accumulator concept introduced in Program 3.5; it demonstrates how values extracted during
matching can be used in arithmetic. Initially, the accumulator is zero (1). If
the input list is empty, then the result is the contents of the accumulator (2).
If the input is not empty, then the result is the obtained by adding the first
element x and the sum of the rest of the list into the accumulator (3). Thus a
program call sum([3,5,6,7],result) defines result to be 21.

The program metric corresponds to the length of the input list Ls; termination occurs when this length is reduced to zero.

Consider, the following composition of programs, similar to that employed
by the min4 program described in Section 2.3:

$$\{ |\, | \text{ generator}(5,L), \text{ sum}(L,\text{result}) \}$$

This composition is intuitively clear from our understanding of the component
programs: The generator creates a list of values [5,4,3,2,1] and the sum program adds up the values to form the result 15. Recall, from Chapter 2, that
a parallel composition terminates when all of its constituent programs terminate. We have argued that both the generator and sum programs terminate;
thus the parallel composition will eventually terminate.

We have discussed how a definition statement forms an abstraction for
sending a message. Previously, in the min4 program, the concept was used to

communicate a single value from one program to another. In the above composition, lists enable *many* values to be communicated between the constituent programs; as execution proceeds, the list is gradually constructed. A list used in this manner we term a **stream**: it gradually trickles from one program to another as shown in Figure 3.1.

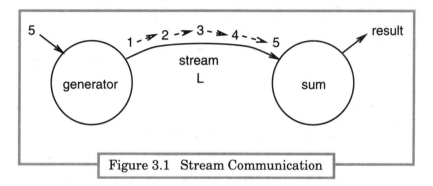

Figure 3.1   Stream Communication

3.2.4   Reversing a List

Specification: Write a program reverse(Ls,Rs) that accepts a list Ls and generates a list Rs; Rs contains all of the elements of Ls in reverse order.

```
reverse(Ls,Rs) rev(Ls,[ ],Rs)                    /* 1 */

rev(Ls,Acc,Rs)
{ ? Ls ? = [ ] -> Rs=Acc,                        /* 2 */
     Ls ? = [x | Ls1]  -> rev(Ls1,[x | Acc],Rs)   /* 3 */
}
```

Program 3.7 Reversing a List

Program 3.7 uses a technique similar to that used to accumulate a sum in Program 3.6; however, in this case the accumulator is a list rather than a number. Initially, the accumulator is an empty list (1). If the input list Ls is empty, then the result is the accumulator (2). Otherwise, Ls is separated into two parts corresponding to the first element x and the rest of the list Ls1 (3). The first element is placed at the beginning of the accumulator and the rest of the list is added in front of it recursively (3). Thus a call reverse([1,2,3,4],Result) defines Result to be [4,3,2,1]. The program metric is the length of the input list Ls; termination occurs when this length is reduced to zero.

3.2.5 Member

Specification: Write a program member(x,Ls,result) that accepts a value x and a list Ls as input. It defines result to be true if x is an element of Ls and false otherwise.

Program 3.8 is a naive solution to the problem that involves multiple tests in the guard of an implication. A guard containing multiple tests is executed as follows:

Guard Execution: Tests are executed from left to right textually. If *all* tests are satisfied then the guard is satisfied. If *any* test is not satisfied then the guard is not satisfied. If *any* test cannot be evaluated then the guard as a whole cannot be evaluated.

```
member(x,Ls,result)
{ ? Ls ? = [ ] -> result = "false",                    /* 1 */
     Ls ? = [m | _], x == m  -> result = "true",        /* 2 */
     Ls ? = [m | Ls1], x != m  -> member(x,Ls1,result)  /* 3 */
}
```

Program 3.8 Member of a List

Program 3.8 recursively inspects each element of the input list Ls. If the input list is empty, then x is not an element of Ls and the result is false (1). If the input list is not empty *and* its first element is equivalent to x, then x is an element of Ls and the result is true (2). If the input list is not empty *and* the first element is not equivalent to x, then it is necessary to determine if x is contained in the rest of the list; this is achieved using recursion (3). Thus a program call member(2,[1,2,3],result) defines result to be true. In contrast, a call member(7,[1,2,3],result) defines result to be false.

What is the termination condition? There are actually two: They correspond to the presence or absence of x in the input list. The metric, as in our previous examples, is the length of the input list. Either the length decreases to zero, indicating that x is not in the input list, or it decreases to a point where x is found. In either case, the program progresses toward termination.

Program 3.9 is an improved version of Program 3.8 that uses *nested choice*. If the input list Ls is empty, then x is not an element and the result is false as before (1). If Ls is not empty, then another choice is made (2). If the first element in the input list is equivalent to x, then the result is true (3); otherwise, the remainder of the list is inspected recursively (4). This alternative formulation removes the repeated test, used in Program 3.8, to determine if the input is a non-empty list.

```
member(x,Ls,result)
{ ?  Ls ? = [ ] -> result = "false",            /* 1 */
      Ls ? = [m | Ls1] ->                        /* 2 */
         { ?  x == m  -> result = "true",        /* 3 */
              x != m  -> member(x,Ls1,result)    /* 4 */
         }
}
```

Program 3.9 Member with Nested Choice

3.2.6   Difference

Specification: Write a program difference(L1,L2,L3) that accepts two lists L1 and L2. It generates a new list L3 that contains every element of L1 that is *not* contained in L2.

Program 3.10 is a solution to the problem and illustrates how other programs may be used in compositions: The program employs the member program presented in the Section 3.2.5 to detect if an element of the input list L1 is contained in list L2.

```
difference(L1,L2,L3)
{ ? L1 ?= [] -> L3=[],                                    /* 1 */
    L1 ?= [x | L1s] ->                                     /* 2 */
        {| | member(x,L2,r),
            { ? r == "true" -> difference(L1s,L2,L3),      /* 3 */
                r == "false" ->
                    {| | L3=[x | L3s], difference(L1s,L2,L3s) }  /* 4 */
            }
        }
}
```

Program 3.10 Difference Between Lists

If the input list L1 is empty, then the resulting difference L3 is empty (1). If the input list is not empty, then the first element x is removed (2). If x is a member of L2 then it is discarded (3); otherwise, x is added to the output list (4). In either case, the remainder of the input is inspected recursively. Thus a program call difference([1,2,3,4],[2,4,6],L3) eventually defines L3 to be the list [1,3].

The metric in this program corresponds to the length of the input list L1. Termination occurs if the length of L1 is zero. Recall, from Section 3.2.5, that the member program terminates and defines the result r to be either true or false. Thus one implication in the nested choice is eventually selected. *Both* choices involve recursive calls that decrease the length of the input list by one; thus the program progresses toward termination.

3.2.7 Intersection

Specification: Write a program intersection(L1,L2,L3) that accepts two lists L1 and L2. The program generates a new list L3 that contains every element of L1 contained in L2.

This problem demonstrates a useful programming technique, the **difference list**, that allows lists to be constructed in parallel. The central idea is to consider a list as the *difference between* two imaginary points. The points correspond to the *beginning* and the *end* of the list and are represented by definition variables. The list is built by generating portions of it concurrently. Program 3.11 is a solution to the intersection problem that uses the technique.

```
intersection(L1,L2,L3) intersect(L1,L2,L3,[])              /* 1 */

intersect(L1,L2,Lb,Le)
{ ? L1 ?= [] -> Lb=Le,                                     /* 2 */
    L1 ?= [x|L1s] ->
            {|| member_add(x,L2,Lb,Lm),                    /* 3 */
                intersect(L1s,L2,Lm,Le)                    /* 4 */
            }
}

member_add(x,Ls,Lb,Le)
{ ? Ls ?= [] -> Lb=Le,                                     /* 5 */
    Ls ?= [m|Ls1] ->
        { ? x == m -> Lb=[m|Le],                           /* 6 */
            x != m -> member_add(x,Ls1,Lb,Le)              /* 7 */
        }
}
```

Program 3.11 Intersection of Lists

Figure 3.2 illustrates how the intersection program implements its specification. Initially, the intersection is represented by the *difference between*
its beginning L3 and its end [] (1). A sequence of member_add programs are
generated recursively, one for each element x of the input list L1 (3,4). All
member_add programs execute concurrently and each builds a portion of the
output list between the list beginning Lb and some intermediate point Lm (3);
subsequent programs generate the portion of the output list between this point
Lm and the list end Le (4).

Each member_add program inspects the list L2 to determine if it contains x.
If x is contained in the input list Ls, then x is added into a portion of the output
list (6). Otherwise, the remainder of the list is inspected recursively (7). If x is
not contained in the input list, nothing is placed into the output list (5). Thus
a program call intersection([1,2,3,4],[2,4,6],L3) eventually defines L3 to be the
list [2,4].

The termination conditions and metric for the member_add program are
exactly those of the member program in Section 3.2.5. The metric for the
intersect program is the length of the input list L1; termination occurs when
the length of L1 is reduced to zero.

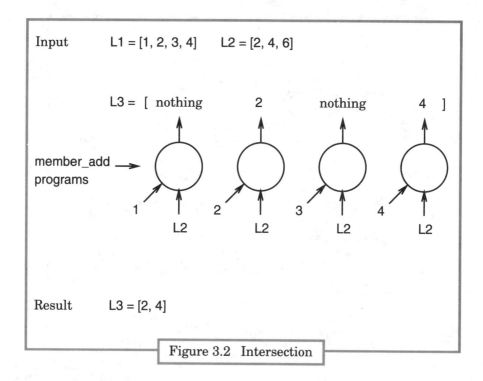

Input   L1 = [1, 2, 3, 4]   L2 = [2, 4, 6]

Figure 3.2   Intersection

3.3   Tree Programs

All of the programs in the previous section manipulated lists. Recall from Section 2.1.1, that we also allow *n*-ary tree structures to be built using tuples. In this section we consider a variety of programs that generate and manipulate these more general structures.

3.3.1   Summing the Leaves

Specification: Write a program sum_tree(T,sum) that computes the sum of the leaves of a binary tree of integers T.

Program 3.12 solves the problem and illustrates a new category of guard test that is used for checking the data type of a value. Figure 3.3 shows how the program propagates information for an input tree {{{1,2},{3,4}},{5,6}}: Leaves pass their value to interior nodes that compute summing operations.

```
sum_tree(T,sum)
{ ? int(T) -> sum=T,                            /* 1 */
     tuple(T) ->                                /* 2 */
          {|| sum=left_sum+right_sum,           /* 3 */
              sum_tree(T[0],left_sum),          /* 4 */
              sum_tree(T[1],right_sum)          /* 5 */
          }
}
```

Program 3.12 Summing Leaves of a Tree

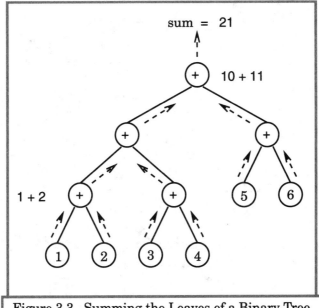

Figure 3.3   Summing the Leaves of a Binary Tree

If the input T is an integer, then it corresponds to a leaf of the tree and the resulting sum is T (1). If the input is a tuple, then it has two component subtrees, T[0] and T[1] (2). In this case, the sum of the leaves in T[0] and the sum of the leaves in T[1] are computed recursively (4,5); the final result is the sum of the leaves in both components (3).

Program 3.13 is an alternative solution using an accumulator. Figure 3.4 shows the flow of information in this formulation. The accumulator is threaded through the tree leaves and summing operations are computed at the leaves.

```
sum_tree(T,sum) sum_tree1(T,0,sum)         /* 1 */

sum_tree1(T,left,right)
{ ? int(T)  -> right=left+T,               /* 2 */
     tuple(T) ->
         {|| sum_tree1(T[0],left,middle),  /* 3 */
             sum_tree1(T[1],middle,right)  /* 4 */
         }
}
```

Program 3.13 Summing with an Accumulator

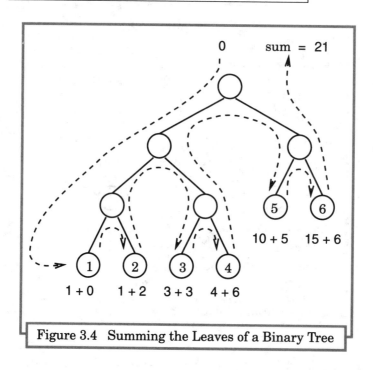

Figure 3.4 Summing the Leaves of a Binary Tree

The accumulator is initially zero (1). If the tree is a leaf, then it is added to the accumulator (2). If the tree is not a leaf, then the accumulator is used to compute the sum of the leaves in the left subtree (3); the result is then used to compute the sum of the leaves in the right subtree (4).

Minor changes can be made to Program 3.13 that allow the accumulator to be threaded via alternative paths. Using the accumulator technique it is also possible, by waiting for values, to implement common tree search algorithms such as depth and breadth first traversal. The resulting formulations effectively implement *stacks* of waiting programs.

Both Programs 3.12 and 3.13 terminate by detection of a integer leaf in the input tree. The metric is the *depth* of the tree. Notice that in every recursive call the depth of the input tree is reduced by one. Termination occurs when the depth is reduced to zero.

3.3.2 Depth of a Tree

Specification: Write a program depth(T,d) that computes the depth d of an arbitrary tree T.

```
depth(T,d)
{ ? tuple(T) ->
          {|| depth_subtrees(length(T)-1,T,d1)         /* 1 */
              d=d1+1                                    /* 2 */
          },
        default -> d=0                                  /* 3 */
}


depth_subtrees(n,T,d)
{ ? n >= 0 ->                                           /* 4 */
          {|| depth(T[n],d2),                           /* 5 */
              depth_subtrees(n-1,T,d1),                 /* 6 */
              { ? d1 > d2 -> d=d1,                       /* 7 */
                  default -> d=d2                       /* 8 */
              }
          },
        default -> d=0                                  /* 9 */
}
```

Program 3.14 Depth of a Tree

Program 3.14 is a solution to this problem and shows how to traverse an arbitrary tree. The program introduces two predefined operations, length and default. The length operation may be used in an expression to compute the number of elements in a given structure. In Program 3.14, it is used to compute the number of subtrees in a tree. The guard test default succeeds when all other guards in a choice are *false*.

If the input tree T is not a leaf, then its depth is the depth of its subtrees (1), plus one (2). If the tree is a leaf, then its depth is zero (3). To compute the depth of a set of subtrees the depth of each subtree is computed recursively (5,6). The depth of a collection of subtrees is the maximum of the depth of the individual subtrees (7,8). Figure 3.5 shows how information propagates in this program. The depth of a leaf is zero and at each subsequent level in the tree, the depth is incremented by one.

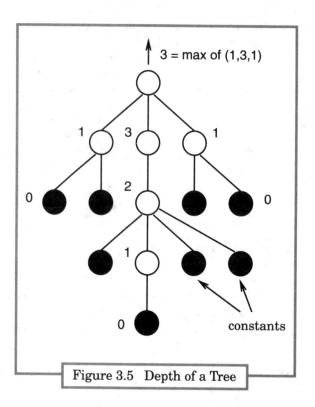

Figure 3.5   Depth of a Tree

Every recursive call to the depth program decreases the depth of the tree by one (5); the program terminates when the depth of the tree is zero (3). Every recursive call to the depth_subtrees program decreases the number of subtrees remaining by one (6); the program terminates when there are no further subtrees to consider (9). Thus both programs terminate.

3.3.3 Generating a Tree

Specification: Write a program rev_tree(T,T1) that accepts
a tree T and outputs a new tree T1. T1 is equivalent to T
except that all subtrees are in reverse order.

This problem demonstrates how trees are constructed. Program 3.15 solves
the problem using a predefined program: make_tuple(n,T). This program is
used to construct a tuple of size n; each element of the tuple is initially undefined.

```
rev_tree(T,T1)
{ ? tuple(T) ->
            {|| n=length(T), make_tuple(n,T1),          /* 1 */
                rev_subtrees(n−1,0,T,T1)                 /* 2 */
            },
        default  -> T1=T                                 /* 3 */
}

rev_subtrees(n,m,T,T1)
    n >= 0 ->
            {|| rev_tree(T[n],SubTree),                  /* 4 */
                T1[m]=SubTree,                           /* 5 */
                rev_subtrees(n−1,m+1,T,T1)
            }
```

Program 3.15 Generating a Tree

If the input tree is not a leaf, the number of subtrees is calculated and a
new tree of the same size is built (1). The arguments of the new tree are built
by reversing the subtrees in the input tree (2). If the input tree is a leaf, the
output tree is unchanged (3).

The program rev_subtrees reverses a set of subtrees by extracting each
subtree from the input tree T in turn. Since the subtree may itself be a tree, it
too is reversed (4). The reversed subtree is placed in the appropriate position
in the new tree (5). Notice how an element of a tuple is defined: It is simply
placed on the left of a definition statement (5).

Every recursive call to the rev_subtrees program decreases the number of
subtrees remaining by one; the program terminates when all subtrees have

been considered. Every recursive call to the rev_tree program decreases the depth of the tree by one; the program terminates when the depth is reduced to zero.

3.4 An Assembler

We end this chapter with a practical programming example involving the core of an assembler:

Specification: Write a program assemble(Is,Os) that takes a stream of instructions Is and generates a stream of values Os representing assembled code bytes. Each instruction is represented in Os by a sequence of four integers p, q, r and s as signified in the following table:

Instruction	p	q	r	s
store(a,value)	1	a	value	0
load(value,b)	2	value	b	0
halt	3	0	0	0
jump(a)	4	address(a)	0	0
label(a)	n/a			

Each assembled instruction corresponds to a unique address in the assembled output Os. The first instruction (all four bytes) corresponds to address 0, the next to address 1, etc. The label instruction causes nothing to be added to the assembled output but records the address a associated with the next instruction in the input. There may be any number of jumps to a single label; these may occur before and/or after the label in the input. The last instruction in the input is always a halt instruction.

Program 3.16 is a solution to this problem and provides a test of your understanding of definitions. The program uses a **prefix form** for denoting tuples whose first argument is a string of characters. For example, the tuple {"store",a,b} is written more conveniently as store(a,b). The solution separates the problem of assembly into two distinct subproblems — *assembling instructions* and *generating addresses* — as illustrated in Figure 3.6.

```
    assemble(Is,Os) {|| asm(Is,As), count(0,As,Os) }              /* 1 */

    asm(Is,Cb)
    { ? Is ? = [store(a,v) | Is1]  ->
            {|| Cb=[{_,1,a,v,0} | Cm], asm(Is1,Cm) },             /* 2 */
        Is ? = [load(v,b) | Is1]  ->
            {|| Cb=[{_,2,v,b,0} | Cm], asm(Is1,Cm) },             /* 3 */
        Is ? = ["halt" | Is1]  ->
            {|| Cb=[{_,3,0,0,0} | Cm], asm(Is1,Cm) }              /* 4 */
        Is ? = [jump(a) | Is1]  ->
            {|| Cb=[{_,4,a,0,0} | Cm], asm(Is1,Cm) },             /* 5 */
        Is ? = [label(a) | Is1]  ->
            {|| Cb ? = [{na,_,_,_,_} | _]  -> a=na,               /* 6 */
              asm(Is1,Cb)
            },
        Is ? = [] -> Cb=[]                                        /* 7 */
    }


    count(n,Is,Os)
    { ? Is ? = [{a,p,q,r,s} | Is1]  ->                            /* 8 */
            {|| a=n, Os=[p,q,r,s | Os1], count(n+1,Is1,Os1) },    /* 9 */
        Is ? = [] -> Os=[]
    }
```

Program 3.16 An Assembler

The asm program implements the task of assembling instructions. If the instruction to be assembled is a store, load, halt or jump, then the appropriate values from the specified table are placed into a message (2,3,4,5). Each message also contains a *hole* that represents the address at which the instruction resides; we do not care where the instructions reside. If the instruction is a label, then the associated address is the address where the next instruction is assembled. To obtain this address we inspect the next instruction (6). If there are no further instructions to assemble, then the message stream is closed (7).

The count program implements an address counter. It receives a stream of messages As containing assembled bytes (8) and numbers each set of bytes with its address. It also generates the assembled output (9). Thus a call

    assemble([load(1,2),label(X),store(3,4),jump(X),"halt"],Os)

defines the stream Os to be Os = [2,1,2,0,1,3,4,0,4,1,0,0,3,0,0,0].

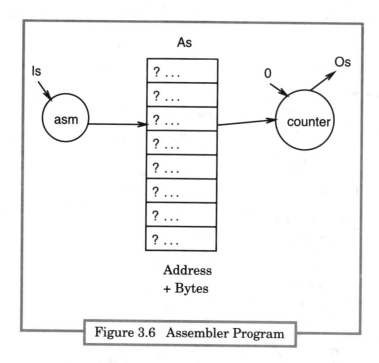

Figure 3.6   Assembler Program

Ensure that you understand how each label, initially represented by a variable, is eventually defined by the assembler.

Every call to the asm program decreases the length of the input Is by one; the program terminates when the length is reduced to zero. Similarly, every recursive call to the count program decreases the length of the assembled data stream by one; the program terminates when the length is reduced to zero. The assembler terminates when both the asm and count programs terminate.

3.5   Summary

In this chapter we have explored four concepts in a variety of programming problems: *definitions, recursion, choice* and *parallel composition*. In general, we have relied on your intuition in explaining how the programs operate and in asserting that the programs implement their specification. In reasoning about a program, we have considered its operation in isolation from all programs with which it is composed. Our ability to do this is a direct consequence of the use of definition variables.

In the course of programming we have used a variety of metrics to reason about program termination. Some of our metrics were explicit, such as a number used in counting arguments; others were obvious implicit metrics, such as the length of a list or the depth of a tree. For the most part we have considered the progress of a program toward termination by inspecting recursive calls and checking that an appropriate metric is decreasing.

Finally, we have seen how programs composed in parallel communicate via streams, synchronize on the availability of data, and terminate when all constituent programs terminate.

Exercises

1. Write a program superpower(x,y,r) that raises x to the power x, y times and defines r to be the result.

2. Write a program generator(n,L) that accepts a positive integer n and generates a list of integers L in the sequence n−1,n−2,...,0.

3. Execute the composition {|| generator(5,L), sum(L,result) } by hand using the techniques introduced in Chapter 2. Convince yourself that the expected result is achieved irrespective of the order in which the programs execute.

4. Write a recursive program svadd(S,V,R) that accepts a scalar value S and a vector V (represented as a list). The program adds the scalar to each element of the vector and defines R to be the result.

5. Rewrite the difference program using the *difference list* programming technique.

6. Write a recursive program vm(V1,V2,R) that accepts two vectors, V1 and V2 (represented as lists), and defines R to be the result of multiplying them.

7. Write a recursive program append(L1,L2,L3) that appends list L2 to list L1 and defines L3 to be the result.

8. Write a program set(L,L1) that returns the set of elements L1 in list L by removing repeated elements in L.

9. Write a program generator(n,L) that accepts an integer n and generates a list of n lists. Each list contains the sequence n−1,...,0.

10. Write a program flatten(T,L) that takes a tree and flattens it into a list. For example, if T is {{{1,2},3},{4,5,6}}, then L is defined to be [1,2,3,4,5,6].

11. Write a program double(T,T1) that takes a tree T and generates a new tree T1. T1 is equivalent to the tree T except that every number in T is doubled in T1.

12. Write a program substitute(x,y,T,T1) that substitutes the value x for every occurrence of the value y in tree T and returns a new tree T1 as a result.

For example, substitute("foo",1,{1,{2,3},{{1}},1},T1) defines T1 to be the tree {"foo",{2,3},{{"foo"}},"foo"}.

13. Write a program merge(S1,S2,S3,Out) that accepts messages on three input streams, S1, S2, and S3, and generates a single stream of messages Out. Any message that occurs on any one of the input streams is transferred to the output stream Out.

14. Write a program integrate(A,B,Result) that computes the integral of the function $x^2 + 7$ over the closed interval A–B. You may include or exclude the points A and B from the interval; this consideration is irrelevant to the method of problem solution.

15. Extend the assembler to return the number of bytes in the resulting output stream Os.

16. Extend the assembler to add *conditional jumps* and *arithmetic operations* of your own specification.

17. Modify the assembler to load and store *four-byte* values.

CHAPTER

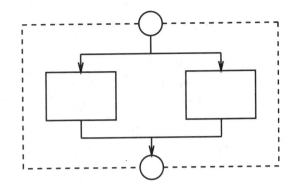

4

Sorting Examples

Goals for this Chapter:

At the end of this chapter you should understand the concept of *algorithm* and be able to recognize more difficult metrics.

In this chapter we solve a single programming problem using four different methods, or **algorithms**:

Specification: Write a program sort(Xs,Ys) that accepts a list of numbers Xs and generates a list of numbers Ys. Ys is a permutation of Xs and Ys is in *ascending order*. Therefore, each element of Xs is contained in Ys and Ys contains only elements of Xs.

For example, a call to a sort program of the form sort([5,3,5,2,1,4,1],Ys) terminates with the variable Ys defined to be the list [1,1,2,3,4,5,5].

Each algorithm that we describe has different properties and works in a completely different manner. The algorithms use more difficult metrics than those we have discussed in previous chapters.

4.1 Insertion Sort

The first algorithm we will consider is called insertion sort. The algorithm considers each element of the input in turn. At each step, an element of the input is *inserted* into its correct place in the output as shown in Figure 4.1.

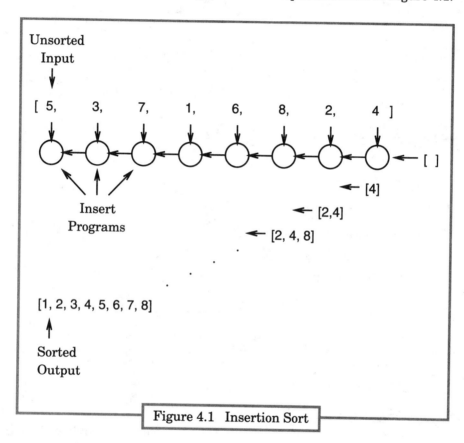

Figure 4.1 Insertion Sort

Program 4.1 implements the sorting specification using the insertion sort algorithm. Initially, an insert program is generated for each element of the unsorted input (1). The last sort program generates an initially empty, sorted output list (2). Each insert program places a single value from the unsorted input into the sorted output. This is achieved by searching the sorted output Zs for the correct position, in ascending order, one element at a time (3). If the element to be inserted is less than or equal to the first element of the sorted output, then the correct position has been found and the element is added to the output (4). Otherwise, the first element of the output remains unchanged and the program continues to search the rest of the sorted output (5). If the

end of the sorted output is reached during insertion, then the value is inserted
at the output end (6).

```
sort(Xs,Ys)
{ ? Xs ?= [x | Xs1] -> {|| sort(Xs1,Zs), insert(x,Zs,Ys) },     /* 1 */
    Xs ?= [] -> Ys=[]                                            /* 2 */
}

insert(x,Zs,Ys)
{ ? Zs ?= [z | Zs1] ->                                          /* 3 */
        { ? x <= z -> Ys=[x | Zs],                              /* 4 */
            x > z -> {|| Ys=[z | Ys1], insert(x,Zs1,Ys1) }      /* 5 */
        },
    Zs ?= [] -> Ys=[x]                                          /* 6 */
}
```

Program 4.1 Insertion Sort

Does the program terminate? The insert program terminates for reasons similar to the member program described in Section 3.2.5. There are two
termination conditions corresponding either to finding the correct place to insert an element in the sorted output, or reaching the end of the list. The metric
is the length of the sorted output list Zs. The sort program also terminates;
the termination condition is the end of the unsorted input and the metric is
the length of the unsorted input. Notice that in both programs the associated
metric is decreased at every recursive call.

Is the program correct? Every element of the input is added to the
sorted output, either in the middle (4) or at the end (6). Initially, the sorted
output is empty and thus is trivially in ascending order. Every insert program
takes a sorted output and adds an element at a position that *keeps the list in
ascending order*. Thus the output list begins sorted, and at every step of the
algorithm it *remains* sorted. Thus, when the program terminates, the output
is sorted and contains every element of the unsorted input.

4.2 Bubble Sort

The bubble-sort algorithm is a completely different method for solving the
same sorting problem. The central concept is to repeatedly reverse any pair
of numbers that is out of order as shown in Figure 4.2. At each step the

entire unsorted input is scanned. If any pair of adjacent numbers is out of order, then they are reversed. The process continues until no pairs are flipped in any traversal of the input. Notice how numbers gradually move to their appropriate position in the sorted output list.

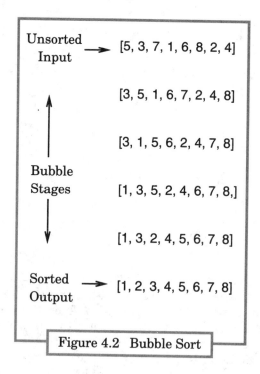

Figure 4.2   Bubble Sort

Program 4.2 implements the bubble-sort algorithm and consists of two program components, *sort* and *flip*. The flip program implements the specification:

Specification: flip(Ls,Ss,R). Accepts a list of numbers Ls and generates a list of numbers Ss. All descending pairs in Ls are reversed to be in ascending order in Ss. The program defines R to be 1 if any pair in Ls is reversed in Ss; otherwise, R is defined to be 0.

The sort program repeatedly applies the flip program to the unsorted input until no elements are reversed (1). If the flip program defines flipped to be a non-zero value, then at least one pair of numbers has been reversed and the flip program is re-applied (2). Otherwise, the sorted output is generated (3).

```
sort(Ls,Ss)
{|| flip(Ls,Ss1,flipped),                                       /* 1 */
      { ? flipped != 0 -> sort(Ss1,Ss),                         /* 2 */
        default -> Ss=Ss1                                       /* 3 */
      }
}

flip(Ls,Ss,R)
{ ? Ls ? = [x,y | Ls1] ->                                       /* 4 */
        { ? x <= y -> {|| Ss=[x | Ss1], flip([y | Ls1],Ss1,R) },   /* 5 */
            x > y -> {|| Ss=[y | Ss1], R=1, flip([x | Ls1],Ss1,_) }  /* 6 */
        },
        default -> {|| Ss=Ls, R=0 }                             /* 7 */
}
```

Program 4.2 Bubble Sort

The flip specification is implemented by recursively inspecting the unsorted input Ls. If the input contains at least two values, then the values are compared (4). If the two numbers are in increasing order, then the first is placed in the output list and the remainder is flipped (5). If they are in descending order, then the second is placed first in the output list and the remainder is flipped (6). If the input contains zero or one numbers, then the input is transferred to the output unchanged (7).

The flip program uses a result argument R to indicate if any pair of numbers in the input is flipped in the output (1). If any pair of numbers is reversed in the output, then R is defined to be one (6); otherwise, it is eventually defined to be zero (7). Notice that many concurrent executions of the flip program may be in progress.

Does the program terminate? It is relatively straightforward to determine that the flip algorithm terminates. The termination condition occurs when the length of the input is either zero or one; the metric is the length of the unsorted input.

It is more difficult to be sure that the sort program terminates. The metric we use is the *number of numbers that are in their final position at the right of the output list*. Notice from Figure 4.2, that each invocation of the flip program moves at least one number to its correct position at the right of the sorted output. For example, in the first step, the number 8 is moved to its correct position; in the second step, the number 7 is moved to its correct position. In all subsequent executions of the flip program this number remains in position. For example, after the first step, the number 8 never moves; after the second step, the number 7 never moves. Thus the number of numbers that are in their final position at the right of the output list gradually increases. When the number of numbers in their final position is equal to the number of numbers in the unsorted input, flip terminates and defines R to be a non-zero value; this allows the sort program to terminate.

Is the program correct? From our discussion of termination criteria, it is clear that each execution of the flip program decreases the number of numbers that are out of their final position. When this number reaches zero, by definition, all numbers are in ascending order. Furthermore, the output list of flip is a permutation of the input list.

4.3   Quick Sort

Figure 4.3 shows the central idea of divide-and-conquer used in the quick-sort algorithm.

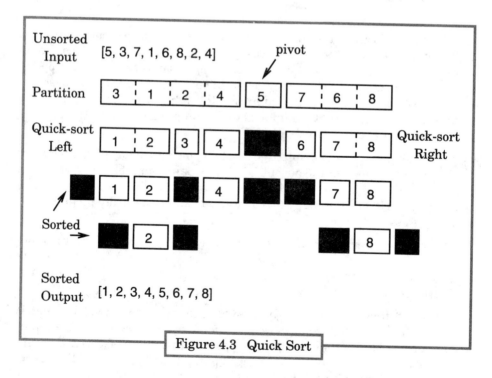

Figure 4.3   Quick Sort

At each step in the algorithm an element from the unsorted input is chosen at random; this number we term the *pivot*. The input is then *partitioned* around the pivot. This involves placing all numbers less than or equal to the pivot on the left and all numbers greater than the pivot on the right. Each partition is then sorted. For convenience, we will always choose the pivot to be the first element of the unsorted input as shown in Figure 4.3.

```
sort(Xs,Ys) qsort(Xs,Ys,[])

qsort(Xs,Yb,Ye)
{ ? Xs ?= [] -> Yb=Ye,                                  /* 1 */
    Xs ?= [pivot | Xs1] ->                              /* 2 */
        {|| part(pivot,Xs1,Left,Right),                 /* 3 */
            qsort(Left,Yb,[pivot | Ym]),                /* 4 */
            qsort(Right,Ym,Ye)                          /* 5 */
        }
}

part(p,Xs,L,R)
{ ? Xs ?= [] -> {|| L=[], R=[]},                        /* 6 */
    Xs ?= [n | Xs1] ->                                  /* 7 */
        { ? n <= p -> {|| L=[n | L1], part(p,Xs1,L1,R)},  /* 8 */
            n > p -> {|| R=[n | R1], part(p,Xs1,L,R1) }   /* 9 */
        }
}
```

Program 4.3 Quick Sort

Program 4.3 implements the quick-sort algorithm using the difference list concept described in Section 3.2.7. If the unsorted input is empty, then nothing is placed in the sorted output (1). If the unsorted input is a sequence of numbers, then the first number is removed and used as the pivot (2). The remainder of the unsorted input is partitioned into a Left and Right part based on the pivot (3). The parts are then sorted recursively (4). The final output is the list between Yb and Ye.

If the unsorted input is empty, then the partitions are empty (6). Otherwise, the partitioning algorithm inspects each element of the unsorted input and compares it with the chosen pivot (7). If the value at the beginning of the list is less than or equal to the pivot, then it is placed in the left partition (8); otherwise it is placed in the right partition (9). In both these cases, the remainder of the unsorted list is added to a partition recursively.

Does the program terminate? Clearly the part program terminates: The metric is the length of the unsorted input; the program terminates when this value is reduced to zero. The quick-sort program also terminates. Notice that a single element is removed from the input every time a qsort program executes. Thus the total length of the left and right partitions always decreases by one.

Is the program correct? As in the case of bubble-sort, we use the concept of the number of numbers in their final position to check that the program operates correctly. Each invocation of the quick-sort program places a single number in its correct position. Figure 4.3 shows how the program progresses. At the first step, a single number is placed in its correct position; at the second step, two numbers are placed in their correct positions, etc. Thus, at each step the number of numbers in their correct position increases; eventually, the program terminates when all numbers are in ascending order.

4.4 Merge Sort

Figure 4.4 illustrates how the merge-sort algorithm operates. The basic idea is to recursively split the input into sublists until each sublist contains at most one element; each sublist is thus sorted trivially. Each consecutive pair of lists is then *merged* to build a larger list that *remains* sorted.

Unsorted Input	[5,3,7,1,6,8,2,4]	
	[5,7,6,2] [3,1,8,4]	split
	[5,6] [7,2] [3,8] [1,4]	split
	[5] [6] [7] [2] [3] [8] [1] [4]	split
	[5,6] [2,7] [3,8] [1,4]	merge
	[2,5,6,7] [1,3,4,8]	merge
Sorted Output	[1,2,3,4,5,6,7,8]	merge

Figure 4.4   Merge Sort

Program 4.4 implements the merge-sort algorithm. If the input contains zero or one element, then the output is the same list (4). Otherwise, the input is split into two parts L and R. Each part is sorted (2) and the two sorted sublists are merged to form the sorted output Ys (3).

```
sort(Xs,Ys)
{ ? Xs ?= [u,v | Xs1] ->                                    /* 1 */
        {|| split(Xs,L,R), sort(L,L1), sort(R,R1),          /* 2 */
            merge(L1,R1,Ys)                                 /* 3 */
        }
    default -> Ys=Xs                                        /* 4 */
}

split(Xs,L,R)
{ ? Xs ?= [u,v | Xs1] ->                                    /* 5 */
        {|| L=[u | Ls], R=[v | Rs], split(Xs1,Ls,Rs) },     /* 6 */
    default -> {|| L=Xs, R=[]}                              /* 7 */
}

merge(L1,L2,L3)
{ ? L1 ?= [] -> L3=L2,                                      /* 8 */
    L2 ?= [] -> L3=L1,                                      /* 9 */
    L1 ?= [x | L1s], L2 ?= [y | L2s] ->                     /* 10 */
        { ? x <= y -> {|| L3=[x | L3s], merge(L1s,L2,L3s) },  /* 11 */
            x > y -> {|| L3=[y | L3s], merge(L1,L2s,L3s) }    /* 12 */
        }
}
```

Program 4.4 Merge Sort

The split program removes elements from the unsorted input two at a time (5). Each time two elements are removed, one element is placed into the sublist L and the other in the sublist R (6). If there are less than two elements in the unsorted input, the remainder are placed into the sublist L (7).

The merge program is responsible for merging a single pair of lists into one larger list. It accepts two lists of numbers in ascending order and produces a single output list, also in ascending order. If either input list is empty, then the output list is simply the other list (8,9). If both lists are non-empty, then the first element of each list is selected (10). The smallest of the two values is moved to the output and the remainder of the corresponding list is merged recursively (11,12).

Does the program terminate? Consider the merge program. Here the metric is the total length of both input lists. At every recursive call this length is decreased by one. Termination occurs when either list has length zero.

Now consider the split program. Here again, the metric is the length of the input list. At every recursive call this length is decreased by two since two elements are removed. The program terminates when the length is reduced to less than two. Note that if the length of the input is two or more elements, then the length of each output sublist is always decreased compared to the length of the input.

Now consider the sort program. Here again, the metric is the length of the input list. Termination occurs when the length of the input is reduced to zero or one. If the input contains two or more elements, then the split program terminates and ensures that at every recursive call the length of the input is reduced.

Is the program correct? Through successive splitting, the input is reduced to sublists containing zero or one elements; these sublists are trivially in ascending order. Whenever two lists are merged, every element of the two component sublists is contained in the result list, only these elements are present and the result is maintained in ascending order. Thus when the program terminates, the final resulting list is a permutation of the input and is in ascending order.

4.5   Summary

In this chapter we have discussed four different algorithms, all of which solve the sorting problem. In checking our programs we have employed metrics that were based on observations of how the algorithms operate. In each case we inspected the program to check both that the program terminated and that the final result was correct.

Exercises

1. A naive sorting algorithm involves generating *all* permutations of the input and then selecting only that permutation that is in ascending order. Design a program that implements this algorithm. Present arguments that show your program terminates and is correct.

2. The odd–even transposition-sort is similar to bubble-sort but flips odd and even pairs in parallel. Design a program that implements this algorithm. Present arguments that show your program terminates and is correct.

CHAPTER
5

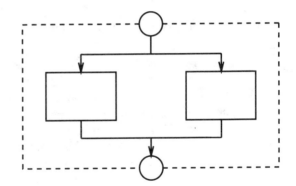

Stepwise Refinement

> **Goals for this Chapter:**
>
> At the end of this chapter you should be able to gradually develop a program using a method termed *stepwise refinement*.

In this chapter we consider a single programming problem involving the design of a simple spreadsheet program. The program is gradually developed from an initial specification through a sequence of *refinement steps*. At each step, the main components of the program are outlined abstractly in order to separate seemingly interrelated aspects of the design. The abstract statements are then incrementally refined until eventually programming constructs are used. The final design is complete when all abstract statements have been removed.

One aspect of this process is that it is frequently possible to make mistakes in the design. This occurs as a result of clarifications that become apparent as the design progresses. In these cases, we backtrack in the design process to a point where the error can be corrected and then continue refinement from that point. Thus backtracking is an integral part of the design process.

5.1 The Problem: A Spreadsheet

Specification: Write a program spreadsheet(n,m,ls) that generates a spreadsheet containing n rows and m columns of cells. The content of each cell is initially the value zero. Each row and column in the spreadsheet has an associated running total. The input stream ls contains a sequence of messages of the form add(x,y,v) or sub(x,y,v). These messages inform the spreadsheet to update the content of the cell at row x and column y by either adding or subtracting respectively the value v.

Figure 5.1 shows the conceptual organization of our solution to the spreadsheet problem. Every cell in a given row is connected to its neighbors; the rightmost cell on a row is connected to a running total. Likewise, every cell within a column is connected to its neighbors and the base cell is connected to a running total. Every cell in the spreadsheet receives messages via the input stream ls.

5.2 Initial Spreadsheet Outline

```
spreadsheet(n,m,ls) {|| totals(...), totals(...), columns(...) }    /* 1 */

totals(...) not_done  -> {|| total(...), totals(...) }              /* 2 */

columns(...) not_done  -> {|| column(...), columns(...) }           /* 3 */

column(...) not_done  -> {|| cell(...), column(...) }               /* 4 */
```

Program 5.1 Initial Spreadsheet Outline

Program 5.1 is an initial outline of the program. The spreadsheet is *composed* of two sets of totals and a set of columns (1). Each set of totals is generated recursively (2). The columns in the spreadsheet are also generated recursively, one column at a time (3). Finally, the cells in each column are generated recursively, one cell at a time (4).

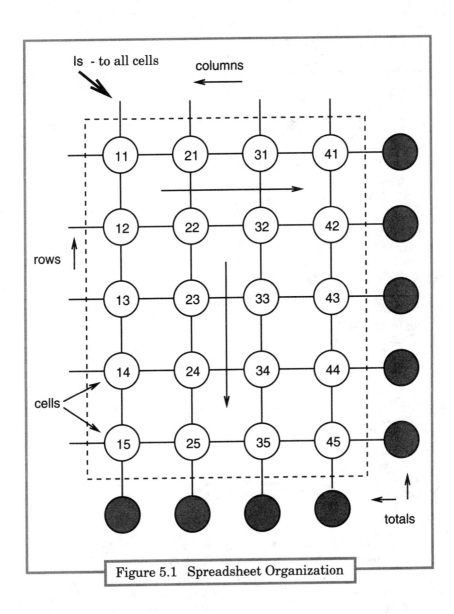

Figure 5.1   Spreadsheet Organization

We now focus on the most difficult aspect of the problem: connecting elements of the spreadsheet. To achieve this refinement, we develop the outline in Program 5.1 to include *streams* that connect cells and totals. The streams are shown in Figure 5.1 and represent paths via which a cell may communicate with a running total. Program 5.2 is a refinement of Program 5.1 that adds this aspect of the design.

```
spreadsheet(n,m,Is)
{|| totals(m,Ws,...), totals(n,Ns,...), columns(Ws,Ns,...) }      /* 1 */

totals(n,Ms,...)
{ ? n > 0 -> {|| Ms=[M | Ms1], total(M,...), totals(n−1,Ms1,...) },  /* 2 */
    default -> Ms=[]
}

columns(Es,Ss,...)
{ ? Ss ?= [S | Ss1] ->
        {|| column(Es,S,Ws,...), columns(Ws,Ss1,...) }            /* 3 */
    Ss ?= [] -> close(Es)                                         /* 4 */
}

column(Es,S,Ws,...)
{ ? Es ?= [E | Es1] ->
        {|| Ws=[W | Ws1], cell(N,E,S,W,...),                      /* 5 */
            column(Es1,N,Ws1,...)
        },
    Es ?= [] -> {|| Ws=[], S=[]}                                  /* 6 */
}

close(Es) Es ?= [E| Es1] -> {|| E=[], close(Es1) }
```

Program 5.2 Connection Refinement

Initially, row totals generate streams to the west and column totals generate streams to the north (1). The number of streams generated is determined by the size of the spreadsheet. As each column is generated, it accepts a set of streams from the east and a single stream from the south; it generates a set of streams to the west (3). As each cell in a column is generated, it accepts a stream from the east and a stream from the south; it generates a stream to the north and a stream to the west (5). Eventually, at the north and west perimeter of the spreadsheet, all streams are closed (4,6).

5.3   Broadcast Refinement

Every cell in the spreadsheet must receive messages via the spreadsheet input stream Is. In order to decide if a message on this stream is destined for the cell, the cell must be identified by its position in the spreadsheet. Program 5.3 refines Program 5.2 to add these aspects of the design. The input stream Is is simply threaded through the program until it arrives at a single cell (1,2,3). Cell numbering is achieved by counting (1,3).

```
spreadsheet(n,m,Is)
{|| totals(m,Ws), totals(n,Ns), columns(n,m,Is,Ws,Ns) }

totals(n,Ms)
{ ? n > 0  -> {|| Ms=[M | Ms1], total(M,...), totals(n–1,Ms1) },
     default  -> Ms=[ ]
}

columns(n,m,Is,Es,Ss)
{ ? Ss ? = [S | Ss1]  ->
          {|| column(n,m,Is,Es,S,Ws), columns(n–1,m,Is,Ws,Ss1) }      /* 1 */
     Ss ? = [ ] -> close(Es)
}

column(n,m,Is,Es,S,Ws)
{ ? Es ? = [E | Es1]  ->
          {|| Ws=[W | Ws1], cell(n,m,Is,N,E,S,W,...),                 /* 2 */
              column(n,m–1,Is,Es1,N,Ws1)                             /* 3 */
          },
     Es ? = [ ] -> {|| Ws=[], S=[]}
}

close(Es) Es ? = [E | Es1]  -> {|| E=[], close(Es1) }
```

Program 5.3 Broadcast Stream Refinement

5.4   Cell Refinement

We now turn our attention to the definition of a single cell in the spreadsheet. Program 5.4 outlines the actions that a cell performs. Each cell has an associ-

ated content, or *state*, and receives messages on the global broadcast stream
ls. If a cell receives a message on the input stream ls, then the message is
inspected (1). If the message is addressed to the cell, then the cell state is
updated, and the operation is forwarded along both the cell's row and column
to the corresponding running total (2); otherwise, the cell disregards the message (3). Messages are forwarded to running totals via other cells on a given
row or column; thus each cell may also receive messages that are in transit.
These messages appear from the north or west and are simply forwarded to
the south and east respectively (4,5). If the input stream ls and both streams
from the north and west close, then the cell terminates, closing its streams to
the south and east (6).

```
cell(...)
{ ? input_message ->
        { ? is_it_for_me ->                                    /* 1 */
                {|| send_to_totals, update_my_content,         /* 2 */
                    cell(...)
                },
            otherwise -> {|| discard_it, cell(...) }           /* 3 */
        },
    message_from_west -> {|| send_to_east, cell(...) },        /* 4 */
    message_from_north -> {|| send_to_south, cell(...) },      /* 5 */
    end_of_all_messages -> terminate                           /* 6 */
}
```

Program 5.4 Outline of a Cell

To complete the design of the cell we simply refine the program by replacing
each abstract operation with the appropriate programming statement. Program 5.5 refines Program 5.4 to complete the design of a cell in the spreadsheet.

5.5 Running Total Refinement

The only remaining aspect of the program is the design of the running total.
This program is sufficiently simple that it can be written directly as shown in
Program 5.6. Each total receives messages originating at cells in the spreadsheet. These messages cause the total to be updated. If the stream of messages
ends, the running total terminates.

```
cell(n,m,Is,N,E,S,W,state)
{ ? Is ? = [{op,x,y,v} | Is1] ->
        { ? x == n, y == m, op == "add" ->
                {|| S=[add(v) | S1], E=[add(v) | E1],
                    cell(n,m,Is1,N,E1,S1,W,state+v)
                },
            x == n, y == m, op == "sub" ->
                {|| S=[sub(v) | S1], E=[sub(v) | E1],
                    cell(n,m,Is1,N,E1,S1,W,state-v)
                },
            default -> cell(n,m,Is1,N,E,S,W,state)
        },
    W ? = [msg | W1] -> {|| E=[msg | E1], cell(n,m,Is,N,E1,S,W1,state) },
    N ? = [msg | N1] -> {|| S=[msg | S1], cell(n,m,Is,N1,E,S1,W,state) },
    W ? = [], N ? = [], Is ? = [] -> {|| E=[], S=[]}
}
```

Program 5.5 Cell Refinement

```
total(Ms,state)
{ ? Ms ? = [add(v) | Ms1]  -> total(Ms1,state+v),
    Ms ? = [sub(v) | Ms1]  -> total(Ms1,state-v)
}
```

Program 5.6 Running Total Refinement

5.6   Program Termination

Program 5.7 is the final spreadsheet program and draws together refinements developed during the design process. The spreadsheet terminates when all of the columns and totals terminate. The columns terminate when all of the constituent cells terminate. The cells terminate when all of their input streams close. Cells at the north and west edges of the spreadsheet have their north and west streams closed initially. Thus, these cells terminate when the input stream Is is closed. The metric for cell termination is the *total length of all its input streams*. At every recursive call this value is decreased, either by removing a message from the input stream Is or by removing a message from a north or west stream. Eventually, all cells terminate and close their output

```
spreadsheet(n,m,Is) {|| totals(m,Ws), totals(n,Ns), cols(n,m,Is,Ws,Ns) }

totals(n,Ms)
{ ? n > 0 -> {|| Ms=[M | Ms1], total(M,0), totals(n-1,Ms1) },
    default -> Ms=[ ]
}

cols(n,m,Is,Es,Ss)
{ ? Ss ?= [S | Ss1] -> {|| col(n,m,Is,Es,S,Ws), cols(n-1,m,Is,Ws,Ss1) },
    Ss ?= [ ] -> close(Es)
}

col(n,m,Is,Es,S,Ws)
{ ? Es ?= [E | Es1] ->
        {|| Ws=[W | Ws1], cell(n,m,Is,N,E,S,W,0),
            col(n,m-1,Is,Es1,N,Ws1)
        },
    Es ?= [ ] -> {|| Ws=[], S=[]}
}

cell(n,m,Is,N,E,S,W,s)
{ ? Is ?= [{op,x,y,v} | Is1] ->
    { ? x == n, y == m, op == "add" ->
        {||S=[add(v) | S1], E=[add(v) | E1], cell(n,m,Is1,N,E1,S1,W,s+v)},
        x == n, y == m, op == "sub" ->
        {||S=[sub(v) | S1], E=[sub(v) | E1], cell(n,m,Is1,N,E1,S1,W,s-v)},
        default -> cell(n,m,Is1,N,E,S,W,s)
    },
    W ?= [msg | W1] -> {|| E=[msg | E1], cell(n,m,Is,N,E1,S,W1,s) },
    N ?= [msg | N1] -> {|| S=[msg | S1], cell(n,m,Is,N1,E,S1,W,s) },
    W ?= [], N ?= [], Is ?= [] -> {|| E=[], S=[]}
}

total(Ms,state)
{ ? Ms ?= [add(v) | Ms1] -> total(Ms1,state+v),
    Ms ?= [sub(v) | Ms1] -> total(Ms1,state-v)
}

close(Es) Es ?= [E | Es1] -> {|| E=[], close(Es1) }
```

Program 5.7 Final Spreadsheet Program

streams; thus the streams to totals are of finite length and are eventually closed. All totals terminate when the length of their input is reduced to zero; notice that every recursive call decreases this length.

5.7 Summary

In this chapter we illustrated the program design technique of stepwise refinement on a simple programming problem. The program was incrementally developed by adding detail to the program specification. Each component of the program was initially specified by a composition of abstract statements. These statements were gradually replaced by program statements until the design was complete.

Exercises

1. Develop a program mm(A,B,C) that computes the matrix multiplication of A and B to produce a result C.

2. Refine the spreadsheet program to add the following facilities:

   • Multiplication and division operations on the cell states.

   • Cell states that are dependent on *other* cell states.

   • Add a grand_total program to the spreadsheet that computes the combined total of *all* cells.

3. Develop a program grid(m,n) that generates a two-dimensional grid of cells where each cell is uniquely numbered by a single number. Each cell is connected to its neighbors via streams and all boundary streams are closed. Each cell computes and prints the sum of its own number and its neighbors' numbers.

4. Generalize your solution to Exercise 3 to three-dimensional grids by refinement.

5. The triangle problem involves a triangular board of the form:

$$1$$
$$2 \quad 3$$
$$4 \quad 5 \quad 6$$
$$7 \quad 8 \quad 9 \quad 10$$
$$11 \quad 12 \quad 13 \quad 14 \quad 15$$

Initially, the board has a peg in each position except position 5. A peg is removed when another peg jumps over it, as in checkers. The first move that is made consists of the peg in position 12 jumping that in position 8. The problem is solved when a single peg remains on the board and a solution consists of the sequence of moves made to reach a solution. There are 775 solutions. Develop a program program to solve this problem that generates all 775 solutions.

6. Develop a program to solve the four-queens problem. This problem involves a chess table of size 4x4. The problem is to generate all possible placements of queens on the board such that no queen may attack another.

CHAPTER
6

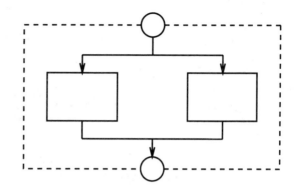

Composing Sequential Programs

Goals for this Chapter:

At the end of this chapter you should understand the concepts of *assignment* and *state*. You should also understand how to compose programs *sequentially*.

In this chapter we briefly review the central concepts involved in sequential programming; a minimal exposure to these ideas via programming in C, Pascal or Fortran is assumed. The concepts are of importance in program refinements concerned with the economy of space and time. Our program development methodology aims to first develop programs without regard to the order in which operations are performed. We subsequently replace program components by components implemented using sequencing while ensuring that the specifications continue to be satisfied.

In general, we adopt the notations and conventions of the programming language C in our treatment of sequential programming. We will use these notations freely and explain any differences that are appropriate.

6.1 Assignment Statements and State

The essence of sequential programming is the organization of updates to **mutable variables**. Each variable corresponds to a *named memory location* whose content can change as the program executes. Variables are created using **declarations**; these indicate the **type** of value the memory location may hold.

The initial value of a mutable variable is not specified; a value is deposited in a variable using an **assignment statement** that is denoted

$$\text{Variable} := \text{Expression}$$

where Expression is an arithmetic expression containing variables and numbers. Some examples of legal declarations and assignment statements are

/* Example Variable Declarations */

int x,y[4];

double a,b[99];

/* Example Assignment Statements */

x := 5

y[3] := ((x+7) − (2*x) / y[3]) % 2

a := 97.3

b[0] := (a+b[57] / 3.142) * 19 * y[0]

The set of all memory locations and their contents, together with the location counters associated with any executing programs, taken at a specific instant in time is called the program **state**.

State: Mutable variables are named memory locations whose initial content is not specified. The content of a variable changes over time by virtue of assignment statements. The *state* of a program comprises the variables, their content and the location counters at a particular instant in time.

6.2   Sequential Composition

Sequential composition is used to signify that programs execute in a particular order, one after the other. We denote sequencing by the composition:

$$\{ \; ; C_1, C_2, \ldots C_n \; \}$$

where each C_i, for $i > 0$, is a composition of programs. This method of composing programs is illustrated in Figure 6.1. On entering the sequential composition, C_1 is initiated. When C_1 terminates, C_2 is initiated. This process continues until C_n terminates, at which point the entire composition terminates.

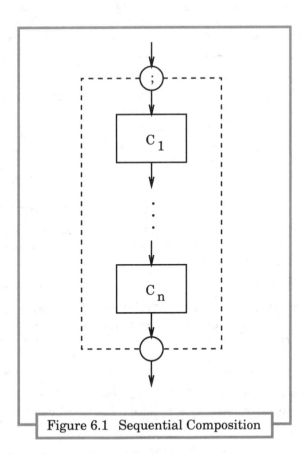

Figure 6.1   Sequential Composition

> **Sequential Composition:** Components are executed in order, one after the other. The composition terminates when the last component terminates.

Sequential programs begin execution in an **initial state**, progress through a sequence of intermediate states and terminate in a **final state**. Transitions between states occur when a program executes an assignment statement or control moves from one statement to another. Thus, our specifications of sequential programs typically involve a description of the initial and final program states. For example:

Specification: Write a program sum(A,s) that accepts an array A of size s. The program begins execution in an initial state total=0 and ends in a final state total=$\sum_i A[i]$.

Program 6.1 is a solution to this problem based on repeatedly updating the variable total. The program illustrates the use of declarations in programs: Any declared variable that is not an argument is created upon program entry as a local variable. Variables persist as long as the program is in execution. Notice from the program comments that to understand the operation of the program, it is necessary to understand the contents of the variables *before* and *after* every statement.

> **Program Transitions:** To understand sequential programs, we must understand the contents of the variables before and after every statement is executed.

As with all of our recursive programs, there is a metric and a termination condition. In Program 6.1 the metric is the value of the variable s and termination occurs when this value is reduced to zero.

> **Metrics in Sequencing:** The concepts of termination condition and metric are equally applicable to sequential programs.

```
/* BEFORE: s=smax=| A |> 0 */

sum(A,s)
double A[ ],total;
int s;
{ ;                          /* total is unspecified */
    total := 0,
                             /* total is zero */
    sum1(A,s,total)
                             /* total is ∑_i A[i] */
}

/* AFTER: total is ∑_i A[i] */



/* BEFORE: 0≤s≤smax, total=∑_j A[j], s≤j<smax */

sum1(A,s,total)
double A[ ],total;
int s;
s > 0  ->
    { ;                      /* 0<s≤smax */
        s  := s − 1,
                             /* 0≤s<smax, total=∑_j A[j], s<j<smax */
        total  := total + A[s],
                             /* total=∑_j A[j], s≤j<smax */
        sum1(A,s,total)
    }

/* AFTER: s=0, total=∑_i A[i] */
```

Program 6.1 Summing Elements of an Array

6.3   Alternative Programming Languages

Specification: Write a program factorial(n,v) that accepts a
positive integer n and sets the value of variable v to n!.

```
factorial(n,v)
int n,v,m;
{ ? n == 0 -> v := 1,                    /* 1 */
     n > 0 ->
          { ;  m := n - 1,               /* 2 */
               factorial(m,v),           /* 3 */
               v := n * v                /* 4 */
          }
}
```

Program 6.2 Factorial Program

Program 6.2 solves the problem using sequential composition. If n is 0, then
v is set to 1 because 0! = 1 (1). If n is positive, then the following statements
are executed sequentially:

1. Set a local variable m to n − 1.

2. Call factorial(m,v); this sets v to m!.

3. Set v to n*v; thus v is n*m! i.e. n!.

The termination condition for the program is n=0. The program metric is
the value of n. If n is initially positive, at every recursive call n is decreased
by one (2). Thus the program progresses toward its termination condition.

Program 6.3 shows a C equivalent to Program 6.2; the two programs are
interchangeable and either may be used as a component in a larger PCN
program. Since C is a sequential programming language, all statements in
Program 6.3 are executed in order. The concept of choice is also used in C via *if*
statements. Although C provides a rich set of parameter-passing mechanisms,
we restrict attention in PCN to call by reference. Notice that the arguments
to the C factorial program are passed as pointers; thus the interface to both
programs is identical and they both compute the same result.

```
        factorial(n,v)
        int *n,*v;
        {  int vn = *n; fact(vn,v); }

        fact(n,v)
        int n,*v;
        {  int m;
           if (n == 0) *v = 1;
             else if (n > 0) {
                 m = n−1; fact(m,v); *v = n*(*v)
             }
        }
```

Program 6.3 Factorial Program in C

Sequential Languages: The language in which a program
is expressed is not important; our understanding of the program is important, not its syntax.

Thus PCN programs may include program components written in any sequential programming language, including C, Fortran and Pascal. This concept
allows PCN programs to utilize existing code libraries.

6.4   Program Design Rules

So far we have presented two distinct views of programming: *parallel programming with definitions* and *sequential programming with assignments*.
To allow these concepts to be used together in a single program, we adopt
three simple rules.

Rule 1: Shared mutable variables must remain constant
during parallel composition.

Consider the composition {|| p(x,y,z), q(x,z) } where x and y are mutable
variables and z is a definition variable. We would like this composition to *mean*

the same thing irrespective of the shared information. This is only problematic in the case of the variable x. If program p executes the assignment x := 5 and program q the assignment x := 6, clearly the value of x is dependent on the order in which p and q execute.

> **Rule 2:** Mutable variables are snapshot, or copied, when used in definitions.

Rule 2 ensures that during a parallel composition, mutable variables act as definition variables; thus the order in which p and q execute is irrelevant. Consider the statement Ys=[x] where Ys is a definition variable and x is a mutable integer variable containing the value 5. This definition is equivalent to Ys=[5] by Rule 2.

> **Rule 3:** When defined, definition variables act as constants in assignment.

Consider the assignment x := x*y+5 where x is mutable and y is a definition variable. Rule 3 states that this assignment may not execute until y is defined and has a numeric value; this value may then be used to evaluate the expression.

Program 6.4 illustrates the use of all three program design rules to solve the following problem:

Specification: Write a program sum3(L1,L2,L3,result) that accepts three lists of numbers L1, L2 and L3. The program defines result to be the sum of all the elements in the three lists.

Notice that the sum3 program is formed using parallel composition (1); the arguments to all of the component programs are *definition variables*. This is the simplest and most frequent application of Rule 1: There are no shared mutable variables and Rule 1 is satisfied trivially. This particular use has the effect of **encapsulating** state change within the sum program. Notice that outside the program, parallel composition and definitions are used; inside the program, sequencing and state change are used. Every sum program may execute in parallel even though internally the program modifies memory.

```
sum3(L1,L2,L3,result)
{|| sum(L1,r1), sum(L2,r2), sum(L3,r3),          /* Rule 1 */
    result = r1 + r2 + r3
}

sum(L,result)
int total;
{ ; total := 0, sum_list(L,total),
    result = total                                /* Rule 2 */
}

sum_list(L,total)
int total;
L ? = [x | Ls]  ->
    { ; total := total + x,                       /* Rule 3 */
        sum_list(Ls,total)
    }
```

Program 6.4 Using Design Rules

Encapsulation: State change can be encapsulated within
parallel programs via Rule 1.

Rule 2 is illustrated by the definition statement result=total where total is
a *mutable* variable (2). This statement causes the definition variable result to
be defined as the value of the variable total by copying. Notice that the use of
sequencing ensures that the result variable is not defined until total contains
the correct value. The final rule is illustrated by the assignment statement
total := total + x. This statement executes only when the definition variable x
has a numeric value. This ensures that the mutable variable total is updated
appropriately.

6.5 Summary

In this chapter we have briefly reviewed the central ideas in sequential program composition. Sequential programming is based on the organization of
updates to named memory locations, or *mutable variables*. To understand how

programs operate, we inspect the content of the memory, or program *state*, before and after every program statement. Assignment statements cause the program state to change, or make a *transition*. Metrics and termination conditions are used to reason about a program's progress toward termination.

Program components expressed in C, Fortran and other languages may be included in PCN programs. This concept allows existing code libraries to be employed in the design of new parallel programs.

Three simple rules are used to define how programs combine the ideas of *parallel programming with definitions* and *sequential programming with mutable variables*.

Part II

Parallel Program Design

CHAPTER

7

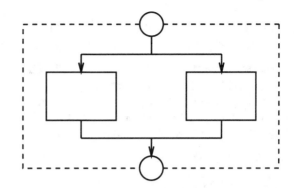

Partitioning, Mapping and Granularity

Goals for this Chapter:

At the end of this chapter you should understand three central parallel programming activities: *partitioning, granularity control* and *mapping*. You should also understand a variety of useful techniques that can be applied to programming problems involving these activities.

In the previous chapters we have focused on writing concurrent programs without concern for how they execute on a specific parallel architecture. We now examine how to take architecture into account by studying three activities: **partitioning** a program into concurrent components, adjusting the **granularity** of these components and **mapping** the components to computers.

There have been numerous attempts to automate these activities, but no practical methods have yet emerged. Fortunately, some general guidelines have evolved that simplify the task of program design. These guidelines are based on a broad classification of programming problems and a variety of programming techniques. Three problem classes can be distinguished: those involving a regular *data domain*, those based on a regular *algorithm* and those *irregular problems* whose primary structure may change as the program executes. Irregular problems are often impossible to partition and map *a priori*;

instead, **load balancing** techniques have evolved that generate partitions and move them between computers during program execution.

In this chapter, we illustrate the classification of problems and describe a variety of useful programming techniques. Simple examples are used to highlight the distinctions between problem classes. In practice, there is often no clear-cut decision, and a combination of programming techniques may be required within a single program.

7.1 Partitioning

The partitioning problem concerns how to break up, or divide, a programming problem into components that may execute concurrently. This does *not* imply a straightforward division of the program into a number of components equal to the number of available computers: Our primary goals in partitioning a program are **scalability** and the ability to **hide latency**.

Scalability concerns how the performance of a given partitioning changes when additional computers are made available. Understanding how a partitioning scales gives an indication of the *maximum* number of computers that can be employed to solve a problem. Figure 7.1 shows a typical performance graph for a parallel program operating on a *fixed-size* problem; it plots time against the number of computers using $\log_2$ scaling. The horizontal dashed line indicates the performance of an equivalent sequential program executed on a single computer.

Initially the parallel program executes more slowly than the sequential program. This difference can be attributed to communication and synchronization overheads that are not incurred by the sequential program. After the parallel program overcomes this overhead, it provides improved performance as the number of computers increases. Eventually, there is a tail-off region where performance does not substantially increase. This region occurs because the problem size is fixed. Eventually, adding computers gains no extra performance, because there is not sufficient work to keep all computers busy.

> **Program Scalability:** The measure of increased program performance for an increased number of computers.

The *minimum* number of components provided by a partitioning is also of interest: We prefer partitionings that provide more components than computers so as to *hide latency*. Latency is the time taken for a message to travel

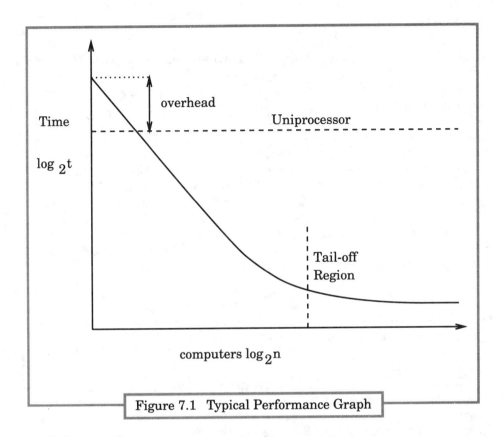

Figure 7.1 Typical Performance Graph

through the architecture and arrive at some destination computer. Typically, a program component will *block*, or wait, if a message carrying needed information has not yet arrived. If other program components are available when blocking occurs, a computer may continue computing even though communication is in progress; this concept, called *multiprocessing*, corresponds to concurrent execution within a single computer and allows aggregate performance to be improved. Thus, at a minimum, partitionings should provide a number of components considerably greater than the number of computers available.

Hiding Latency: Use multiprocessing within each computer to keep computers busy during communication.

We now examine three principal partitioning strategies: domain decomposition, functional decomposition and irregular decomposition.

7.1.1   Domain Decomposition

Domain decomposition is a partitioning technique that has proved valuable for a wide variety of scientific problems. It is useful when a problem is primarily concerned with a large, regular *data domain*. The central idea is to divide the domain, represented by prominent data structures, into components that can be manipulated independently. Examples of these structures include large sparse and non-sparse matrices used in linear algebra, computational grids used in flow dynamics and genetic sequences used in biology. Each component of a partitioning represents a basic unit of computation that will eventually reside at only one computer within the network. For example, suppose a linear algebra problem is dominated by matrix arithmetic on large, non-sparse matrices. A solution of the problem may involve using domain decomposition to partition the matrices into components. Figure 7.2 shows two common forms of decomposition applied to a matrix A: a one-dimensional decomposition into columns (a), and a two-dimensional decomposition into patches (b).

> **Domain Decomposition:** Divide up the *data* of a program and operate on the parts concurrently.

To understand how the matrix components are used, consider the matrix multiplication A x B = C, where the matrix B is partitioned by column as shown in Figure 7.3. To calculate a column of the result matrix C, inner product calculations between the corresponding column of B and each row of A must be performed. These calculations are completely independent and may be computed in parallel.

Clearly, the scalability of this partitioning is governed directly by the number of columns in the matrix B. Provided that the number of computers is less than the number of columns, we would expect to obtain performance improvements when additional computers are made available. For a given *fixed-size* matrix, adding computers will eventually produce no corresponding increase in performance; this corresponds to the tail-off region in Figure 7.1. To obtain further improvements, it is necessary to scale the problem size with the number of computers; this phenomenon has been repeatedly observed in practice.

> **Problem Scaling:** It is often necessary to scale the problem size with the number of computers to maintain performance improvements.

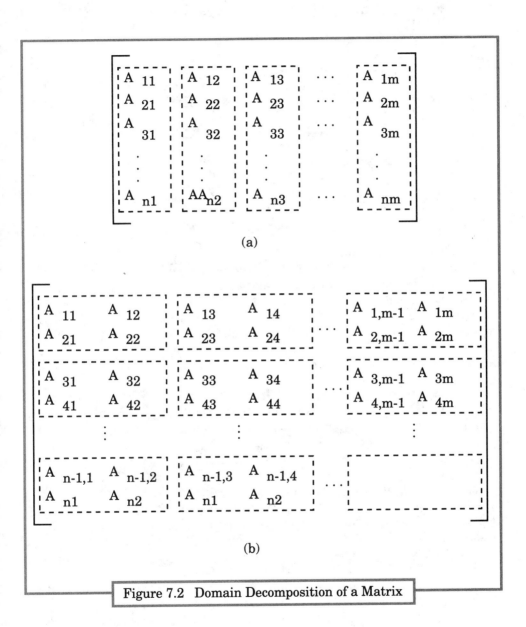

Figure 7.2 Domain Decomposition of a Matrix

$$A\,x\begin{bmatrix} B_{11} \\ B_{21} \\ \vdots \\ B_{n1} \end{bmatrix} = \begin{bmatrix} C_{11} \\ C_{21} \\ \vdots \\ C_{n1} \end{bmatrix} \quad \cdots \quad A\,x\begin{bmatrix} B_{1m} \\ B_{2m} \\ \vdots \\ B_{nm} \end{bmatrix} = \begin{bmatrix} C_{1m} \\ C_{2m} \\ \vdots \\ C_{nm} \end{bmatrix}$$

Figure 7.3   Concurrent Inner-Product Calculations

A wider variety of decompositions is available in problems involving a three-dimensional data domain. For example, in computational fluid dynamics, the flow field of a problem is often represented by a three-dimensional array corresponding to a computational grid. Each cell in the grid represents attributes of the flow, such as the velocity and pressure; these attributes are updated through some iterative scheme based on the value of neighboring cells. This type of structure may be decomposed in one, two or all three dimensions, as shown in Figure 7.4. The shaded areas correspond to a single partition and comprise some number of cells.

There is an implicit assumption in domain decomposition that performance is related to the *size* of the data; moreover, that a regular division of data among computers will yield a regular division of work, circumventing the need for load balancing. Often, however, data decomposition provides only a *starting point* for a program design. Decomposing the data is useful but may have little relationship with the communication patterns involved in solving the problem. For example, in flow dynamics even simple regular grid problems can require sophisticated *communication structures* due to a variety of complications: Some points in the flow field may have unique properties, boundary values may be related mathematically, flow parameters such as the *average pressure* may need to be calculated globally, etc. These constraints may be combined with sophisticated numerical algorithms such as multi-grid or adaptive meshing to produce problems that are algorithmically complex. The division of the data domain in such problems is a relatively minor activity in the overall design. Insight into the structure of the resulting algorithms is required, and the organization of communication and synchronization dominates the design process. The necessary insight can often be attained through performance monitoring and measurement.

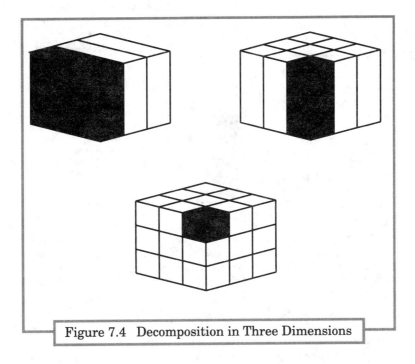

Figure 7.4   Decomposition in Three Dimensions

7.1.2   Functional Decomposition

Functional decomposition is a partitioning technique used where the dominant aspect of a problem is the function, or algorithm, rather than operations on data. The strategy is concerned primarily with dividing up the *function* of a program. For example, consider the problem of computing the integral of some function $f(x)$ on the closed interval $[a, b]$. The basic algorithm involves computing the area under the curve as shown in Figure 7.5. A functional decomposition of the problem would divide the interval into n strips of width w. The area of each strip can then be computed independently and concurrently; the total area is simply the sum of the strip areas. Notice that there is no data to be partitioned; the dominant aspect of the partitioning is the algorithm used to compute area. As in domain decomposition, the computation involved in solving each partition is broadly equivalent and thus no load balancing is required. Scalability depends purely on the number of strips and is analogous to the column-based domain partitioning in Figure 7.2 (a).

> **Functional Decomposition:** Divide up the *function* of the problem and operate on the parts concurrently.

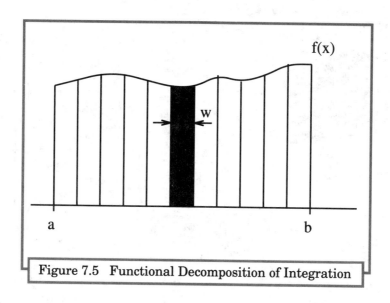

Figure 7.5   Functional Decomposition of Integration

Functional decomposition can lead to algorithmically complex program designs if the components of the decomposition are not similar in execution time and therefore self-balancing. For example, consider the structure of a typical high-level language compiler. To a first approximation, the algorithm involved may be a pipeline similar to that shown in Figure 7.6.

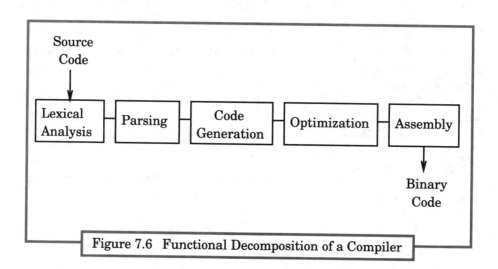

Figure 7.6   Functional Decomposition of a Compiler

There are five primary activities in the pipeline. These correspond to lexical analysis, parsing, code generation, optimization and assembly. A functional decomposition may first focus on a formulation of the problem in which these components execute concurrently. Subsequently, attention may turn to each of the components of the pipeline. In this manner the entire function of the compiler is incrementally decomposed. The use of a pipeline limits the speed of the entire program to the speed of the slowest element, and some insight is required to decide which areas of the pipeline are more significant to overall performance. Again, this insight can frequently be attained through performance monitoring and measurement.

7.1.3 Irregular Problem Decomposition

The dominant aspect of an irregular problem is that the program structure evolves dynamically as the program executes and cannot be determined *a priori*; this may be due to the algorithmic structure of the problem or to a dependence on input data. Problems within this class include irregular adaptive computations in flow dynamics, particle flow simulations, genetic sequence alignment in biology and game-playing programs.

Typically, at the heart of these computations is some graph or tree-like structure that changes dynamically as the program executes. For example, in particle flow simulation, the tree may be an 8-ary tree representing divisions of three space; in game-playing programs such as chess there may be an alpha-beta tree corresponding to board situations. Since the trees evolve as the program executes, they must be partitioned dynamically. Moreover, since the size of the partitions may vary widely, some method of load balancing must be employed to keep computers busy. Figure 7.7 shows two useful strategies for decomposing trees. The first partitioning (a) involves choosing a level in the tree where the number of leaves is large; sub-trees below this level may then be used as program partitions. The second partitioning (b) involves dividing the tree regularly at constant increments in the level. Which scheme to use will depend on the structure of the tree, the cost of computing paths and the load balancing scheme to be used.

A useful technique for partitioning graphs is to first construct a *spanning tree* for the graph as shown in Figure 7.8 (a) and (b). A spanning tree has the property that it contains every node in the graph but no cycles. There are a variety of standard algorithms, such as Kruskal's Algorithm, for computing these trees. The original graph may be decomposed using a tree decomposition from Figure 7.7 to divide the spanning tree.

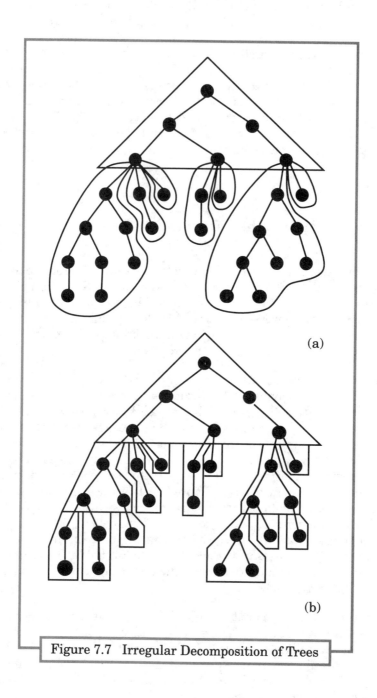

(a)

(b)

Figure 7.7   Irregular Decomposition of Trees

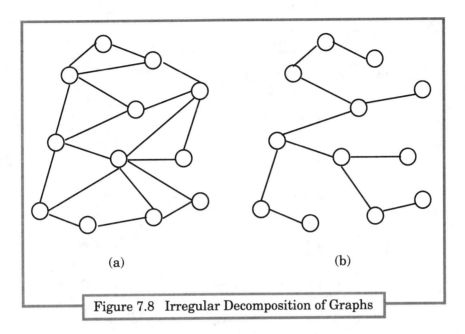

(a)   (b)

Figure 7.8   Irregular Decomposition of Graphs

7.2   Granularity

The granularity of a computation is the ratio of computation to communication. When a programming problem involves regular structures, it is often possible to vary the granularity so as to increase computation or reduce communication. The central idea is to use *locality*: areas of the problem that use the same information are grouped together and executed sequentially to reduce communication.

To illustrate the concept let us reconsider the matrix multiplication partitioning in Figure 7.3. Here the basic unit of computation involved the calculation of a single column of the result matrix C. To achieve this computation all rows of the A matrix must somehow be communicated to the location of a B matrix column. To change the granularity of the computation, we may associate some number m of columns together at a single computer as shown in Figure 7.9. The communication has remained constant: sending the rows of the A matrix. However, the computation that may be performed due to this communication is now m times greater since m columns of the result matrix may now be computed sequentially. Clearly, the same technique can be used to vary the number of cells within the grid partitions shown in Figure 7.4.

The same technique can also be applied to functional decompositions. Consider the integration example shown in Figure 7.5. Here the unit of computa-

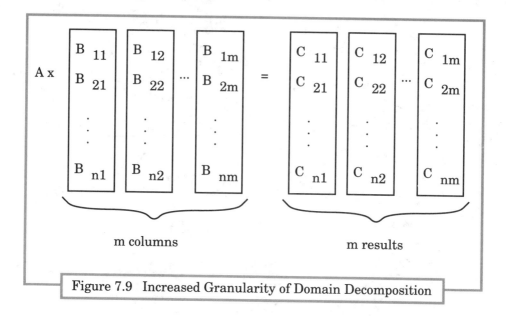

Figure 7.9   Increased Granularity of Domain Decomposition

tion consisted of calculating the area of a single strip in the interval $[a, b]$. To carry out this computation, the location of the strip and the strip width must be communicated to a computer responsible for the calculation. To improve the granularity, m adjacent strips are grouped together as shown in Figure 7.10. The communication required to compute a group of m strips would involve the starting position x of the group, the strip width w and the number of strips in a group m. Since the computation of a single strip area requires evaluation of the function $f(x)$ at each end of a strip, intermediate values can be reused within a group calculation. Thus, for a slight increase in communication (the integer m), m times more work can be computed sequentially; in addition, the computation is more efficient since partial results can be shared.

> **Granularity:** Group partitions to exploit locality thereby increasing the ratio of computation to communication.

This technique is an *optimization* and should be applied with care. Clearly, the concept is only useful if the number of partitions is so much larger than the number of computers available that the additional concurrency cannot be utilized. Programs should be parameterized for an *arbitrary* grain size to yield scalable designs. In the previous examples the value of m would be a parameter used throughout the program whenever granularity is concerned.

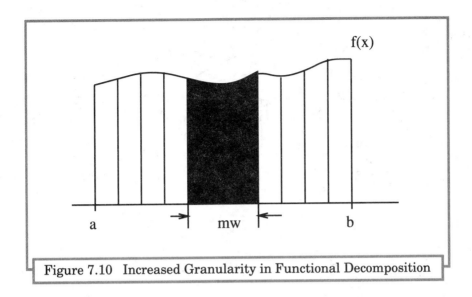

Figure 7.10   Increased Granularity in Functional Decomposition

7.3 Mapping

After a problem is partitioned, the components must be allocated, or *mapped*, to computers for execution. An important aspect in this activity is maintaining locality: placing components of the problem that must exchange information as close as possible within the architecture to reduce communication. Since mapping is concerned with utilizing a particular machine, some details of the architecture are required. For simplicity, we assume the existence of n computers numbered sequentially from zero to $n-1$.

7.3.1 Indexing

The simplest mapping technique, *indexing*, is often used for domain and functional decompositions. The basic idea is to employ some number, or index, used in the problem partitioning; some function of the partition number is then used to allocate a partition to a computer. For example, consider the column partitioning shown in Figure 7.9. Here the allocation problem corresponds to assigning groups of columns, each representing a partition, to computers. A convenient index may be obtained by numbering the groups; a simple allocation function may be the group number *modulus* the number of computers. This produces the round-robin allocation shown in Figure 7.11.

It is instructive to examine the alternative mapping based on integer division shown in Figure 7.12. Here the allocation function is simply the group

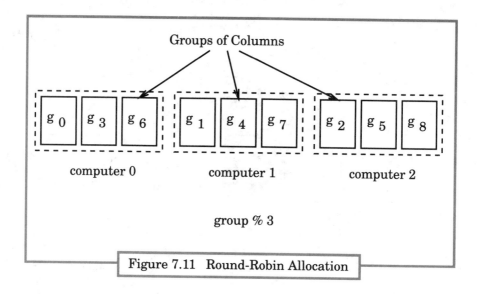

Figure 7.11   Round-Robin Allocation

number divided by the number of computers; thus consecutive groups are packed into the same computer. It may appear that this organization could be obtained by merely increasing granularity as described in Section 7.2. However, if multiprocessing is available at a single computer, then the organization shown in Figure 7.12 is able to cover latency with computation as described in Section 7.1; increasing granularity produces a single sequential program.

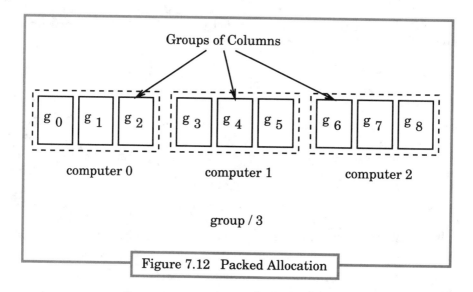

Figure 7.12   Packed Allocation

7.3.2 Hashing

Hashing is a familiar concept from sequential programming. This technique
is particularly useful when the central aspect of a programming problem is
search; however, similar data structures are also used to represent sparse
matrices, and thus the general organizational principles are useful in a variety
of situations. Figure 7.13 shows a hash table representing a database of names
and telephone numbers. The table consists of two parts: an array of size n
and a set of linked lists each associated with an element of the array. Each
entry in a linked list contains a single name and telephone number.

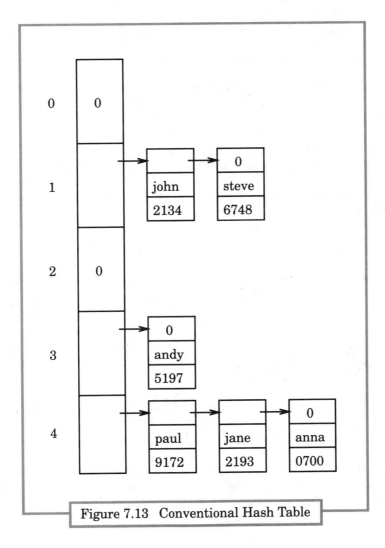

Figure 7.13 Conventional Hash Table

To add an entry to the table, a *hash function* is applied to the name field to produce a *key*; the key is an integer in the range 0 to $n-1$. By indexing into the array, using the key, a specific linked list is chosen and the entry is added to this list if it is not already present. A wide variety of hash functions could be used. In our example, the ASCII characters in the name field are treated as integers, added together, and this value, modulus the array size, is taken as the key. For example, the name *steve* corresponds to the integers 115, 116, 101, 118 and 101, which sum to 551; if the table size is 5, then this name yields a key of 1.

To search for an entry in the table, given a name, the inverse operation is applied. The hash function is applied to the name to yield a key and the list at the key position is extracted; this list is then searched for an entry with the appropriate name. If the hash function is effective in dispersing the entries one per array element, most searches will be achieved in constant time.

The hashing technique can be used in a variety of applications for allocating data and program partitions to computers. To achieve this, the array data structure is replaced by the *array of computers* as shown in Figure 7.14. The hash function is used to decide which computer holds the information of interest. Instead of indexing into the array of lists, communication with a particular computer is used to access information. In this manner, partitions and data can be mapped using the hash function, accesses to the hashed data can be performed concurrently, and, provided that any computer can use the hash function, completely distributed access is possible.

Hashed Allocation: Place information at a computer using a hash function and use communication to access it.

7.3.3 Simulated Annealing

Simulated annealing is an interesting technique that can be used for static physical placement of program components. The central idea is to use a search algorithm to generate trial mappings. A mechanism must be provided to assess the cost, or quality, of a given mapping. As mappings are generated, their costs are examined and mappings with a low cost are accepted. The process continues according to an annealing schedule until all trials are of higher cost than that currently achieved. Unfortunately, this method carries a considerable computational cost and does not appear well suited to problems that are irregular or highly dynamic.

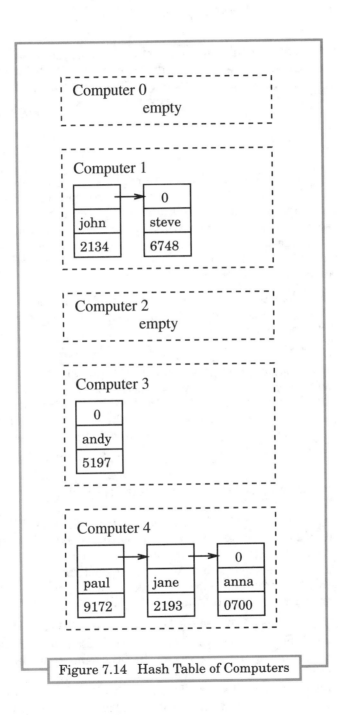

Figure 7.14 Hash Table of Computers

7.4　Load Balancing Techniques

Recall that the central idea in load balancing is to move units of computation between computers as a program executes. The intention is to keep computers busy by balancing the load at each computer. Typically, load balancing is used on irregular problems whose structure evolves dynamically.

7.4.1　Bin Packing

Bin packing is a technique used in cases where partition execution time is proportional to the length of a particular data structure but structures vary in size. The central idea is to pack the data into computers by placing the next data segment at the computer with the *smallest* amount of stored data. To achieve this organization it is necessary to keep track of how much data is allocated to each computer. The goal is to keep the amount of data at each computer balanced and thus balance the computation.

For example, consider a simple problem taken from biology: Compute the number of times a particular piece of DNA exists in a large database of DNA segments. DNA segments are represented as strings over the character set {*a,t,g,c*}, e.g., the substring *aata* occurs twice in the sequence *aaataata*.

One solution is to employ a simple linear matching algorithm to determine the number of times a substring occurs in each DNA segment. Clearly, the total computational time is then related to the total length of all DNA segments. Figure 7.15 shows an example bin packing of substrings for this problem. The length of a substring in this figure is represented by the height of a box; substrings are labeled with numbers and are placed into computers in numerical order.

DNA segments are packed into computers based on the number of characters in a segment. Each computer uses the same matching algorithm to compute the number of matches in its segment of the database. The total time is therefore divided between computers in proportion to the length of substring stored at each. Notice that the quality of load balancing depends largely on the variance in string lengths and the number of strings: Many strings of similar length will produce even load balance; a small number of strings that vary widely produce a poor load balance.

The method is not restricted to statically preallocated loads. For example, if the previous database evolves dynamically as a result of input data, the bin-packing algorithm would be used as the program executes. To achieve this organization it is necessary to be able to compute the *global minimum* throughout the computer network. This provides the ability to dynamically choose where to allocate the next piece of input data.

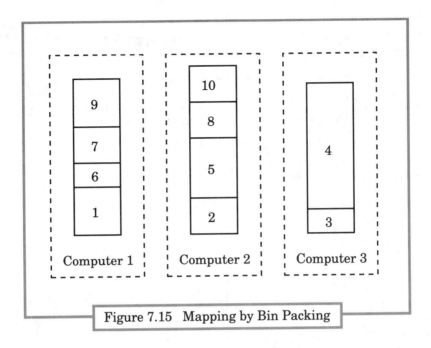

Figure 7.15   Mapping by Bin Packing

Bin Packing: Place a partition at the computer with *least* data.

7.4.2   Randomization

In its simplest form, the concept of *randomized mapping* involves a straight-forward numbering of the computers. Each time a partition must be allocated to a computer, a random number is generated within the computer number-ing range; a partition is then assigned to that computer. The technique can be used for load balancing by allowing every computer to dynamically map partitions using a randomized mapping.

Clearly, the choice of random number generator is of importance in this method. A naive assumption is that a random number generator with a uni-form distribution would produce uniform load balancing and hence higher performance. However, this is not necessarily the case. For example, an al-ternative technique, in one-dimension, is to employ a generator conforming to a bell-shaped curve similar to that shown in Figure 7.16. Here, random numbers represent distance from the current computer in hops to adjacent computers; the curve would generate a greater frequency of allocations closer to the current computer than farther away from it. The same curve would be used by every computer that maps program components; thus, the mapping tends to enhance *locality* and reduce communication.

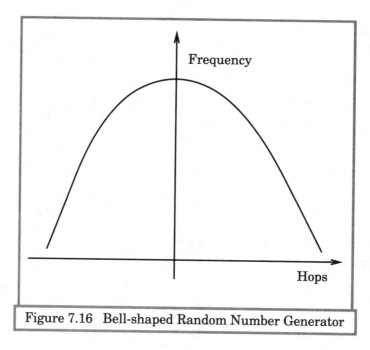

Figure 7.16 Bell-shaped Random Number Generator

Randomization is a general technique that becomes increasingly attractive as the number of computers continues to grow and their cost continues to fall. Consider the situation where a parallel machine contains hundreds of thousands of computers or perhaps millions of computers: Will we care if all computers are fully utilized, any more than we care if main memory is fully utilized today?

> **Randomization:** Load balance by placing partitions at a random computer.

7.4.3 Pressure Models

In pressure models, work is treated as a fluid that flows over the architecture. The quantity analogous to work in flow dynamics is *pressure*. Computers have an internal pressure corresponding to the work to be performed locally and an external pressure corresponding to the work to be performed by other computers. The concept in load balancing is to direct work along pressure gradients to areas of the network that correspond to low pressure, i.e., clusters of computers with low load.

This scheme is simple, requires no global information and is completely distributed. Each computer keeps track of a small number of neighbors and some indication of its own current load, such as the number of runable program partitions available. If the load at a particular computer approaches some critical point, the computer communicates with its neighbors to determine which has lightest load; work is then transferred to that computer. Figure 7.17 shows the movement of a single unit of work as it moves through a mesh; each circle represents a computer and the associated integers represent a measure of current load. Over a period of time, work tends to propagate to areas of the network with least load.

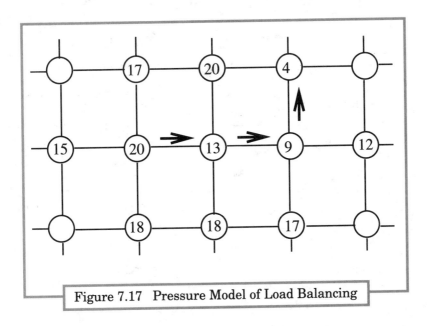

Figure 7.17   Pressure Model of Load Balancing

Pressure Models: Load balance by local movements based on information from neighboring computers.

7.4.4 Manager-Worker

The manager-worker scheme, depicted in Figure 7.18, is a simple centralized scheme that involves a manager program and a collection of workers. The manager is responsible for partitioning a problem into components and allocating the components to workers. Workers are responsible for solving components and are generally assigned to independent computers. When a worker completes the solution of a component it notifies the manager; the manager then allocates a new component. This technique can be used to solve irregular problems where the partitioning yields a tree division similar to that shown in Figure 7.7(a). In this partitioning, the tree is divided at a single level. Each leaf component can be allocated to a worker and solved independently.

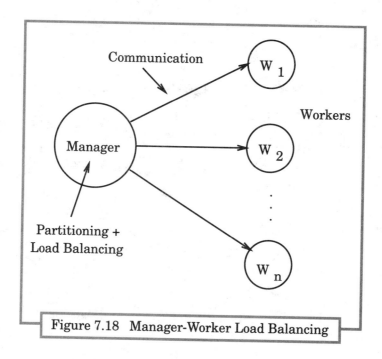

Figure 7.18   Manager-Worker Load Balancing

The basic scheme can be optimized by *buffering* extra work at the workers. Initially, a worker is sent some number of components which it places into a buffer. When removing a component from the buffer, the worker also requests that the manager add additional work to the buffer through communication. Thus, it is possible to *hide latency* in this method by overlapping the communication of one problem component with the computation of others.

> **Manager-Worker:** The manager partitions the problem into components and allocates them to workers; workers compute components.

A variant of the scheme involves allowing the workers to contribute work back to the set of program partitions maintained by the manager. In this scheme, a worker accepts a problem component, works on it for some period of time and then sends any unsolved components back to the manager as shown in Figure 7.19. This scheme can be used with irregular partitionings such as that shown in Figure 7.7(b). In breaking the tree by levels, additional problem components are created that must be reallocated to computers; this is achieved by sending them back to the manager.

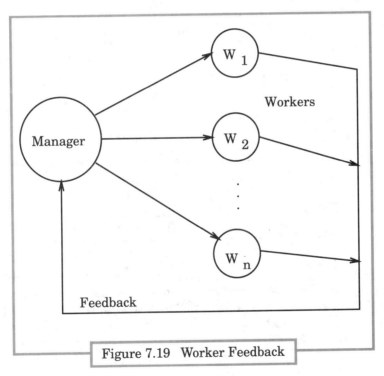

Figure 7.19   Worker Feedback

The manager-worker scheme relies on the fact that the problem can be partitioned into a number of components substantially larger than the number of computers available; a good rule of thumb is at least an order of magnitude. Figure 7.20 shows a typical utilization curve for a problem solved with this technique. Initially, there is a ramp-up period where the machine is under-utilized. This occurs because the manager is partitioning the problem and gradually increasing the number of active workers. When all workers are active, the scheme achieves good utilization for some period. Eventually, there is a ramp-down period because no more problem components are left to be solved; thus, computers begin to sit idle, reducing utilization. Eventually, when all components are solved, the program terminates. For the technique to be effective, the period of full utilization must be long compared to the ramp-up and ramp-down periods; moreover, to decrease the ramp-down time, the size of problem components should not vary considerably.

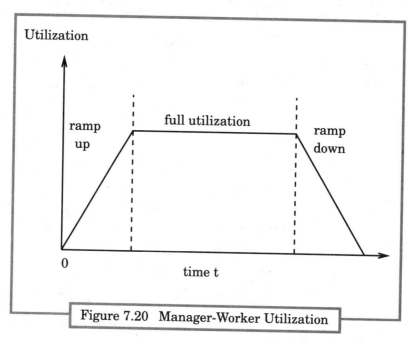

Figure 7.20   Manager-Worker Utilization

Although the technique has been used on a wide variety of problems, it is not particularly attractive from a scalability perspective since it relies on a central manager. Generalizations of the method have been proposed that employ multiple managers to reduce the bottleneck of the single manager. Unfortunately, this organization is complex and has not been used extensively.

7.5 Summary

In this chapter we have described the central parallel programming problems of partitioning a problem into components, controlling the granularity of the components and mapping them to computers. We have suggested that problems fall into three broad categories. The first category contains problems that are concerned primarily with the manipulation of large, regular data structures; these can be decomposed through domain decomposition. The second category contains programs that are primarily concerned with some algorithm; here there is no data structure to be manipulated and attention turns to dividing the algorithm into parts using functional decomposition. Finally, some problems are irregular and must be partitioned dynamically; these typically involve some tree or graph-like structure. We have described a variety of simple but useful techniques that can be employed for mapping and load balancing program partitions.

Exercises

1. What is the difference between domain and functional decomposition? Suggest three problems that fall into each category and explain how the decomposition strategy is applied to each.

2. Outline a parallel matrix multiplication algorithm for multiplying sparse matrices.

3. Describe a parallel Gaussian Elimination program and explain how you might map it to a parallel machine.

4. A camera generates a sequence of 24-bit values corresponding to a color value for each pixel of an image. Outline a program that can be used to scale the size of the image; your program may store only one Nth of the data at each of N computers.

5. Outline a parallel program to play Tic-Tac-Toe. Describe how to map the program to a parallel machine.

6. The triangle problem involves a triangular board of the form:

$$1$$
$$2 \quad 3$$
$$4 \quad 5 \quad 6$$
$$7 \quad 8 \quad 9 \quad 10$$
$$11 \quad 12 \quad 13 \quad 14 \quad 15$$

Initially, the board has a peg in each position except position 5. Pegs are removed by jumping over other pegs as in checkers. The first move that is made consists of the peg in position 12 jumping that in position 8. The problem is solved when only a single peg remains on the board and a solution consists of the sequence of moves made to reach a solution. There are 775 solutions. Outline a parallel program to solve this problem that generates all 775 solutions using the manager-worker load balancing technique.

7. Outline a parallel program that computes addition and subtraction of sparse matrices.

8. Outline a parallel program that implements Kruskal's Algorithm to compute a spanning tree.

9. An accountant keeps two sets of information, one about *customers* and one about *companies*. For each customer, the information comprises the name, address, telephone number, salary and company name where the customer is employed. For each company, the information comprises the company name, address and the name of the managing director.

   To be able to give priority to rich customers, the accountant would like to generate the following:

   (a) A list of all customers who earn more than some specified value.

   (b) A list of all customers that are managing directors of their companies.

   Outline a parallel program that would allow the accountant to generate these lists.

CHAPTER 8

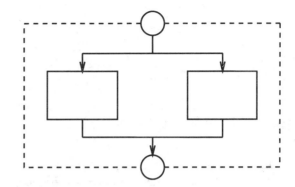

A Regular Grid Problem

Goals for this Chapter:

At the end of this chapter you should understand how to develop parallel programs through stepwise refinement. You should also understand how problems such as partitioning, granularity control, mapping, memory management and code reuse can be separated into specific *refinement steps* and treated independently.

In Chapter 7 we outlined basic methods for partitioning, granularity control and mapping. Although important, these concepts may not be sufficient to obtain an efficient scalable program. Other issues such as memory optimization and the use of existing code libraries may also be factors in the design. Due to the range of alternative solutions for any particular programming problem, it is critical that a methodical program development technique be used.

In this text we have emphasised the use of *stepwise refinement* for program design. We now apply this technique to the solution of a simple grid problem taken from electromagnetic theory: the Dirichlet problem. The program development involves a methodical design from an initial specification through a sequence of refinements. Five critical refinement activities are treated: partitioning the problem into concurrent components, mapping these components to computers, controlling the granularity of computation, efficiently managing memory, and utilizing existing code libraries. The program development demonstrates that these activities can be approached relatively independently, allowing alternatives to be investigated without substantial rewriting of the program text.

8.1   The Problem

The Dirichlet problem deals with a cellular space, as illustrated in Figure 8.1, where the state s of each cell is represented by a single floating-point number. Values are initially given for boundary cells; interior cells initially have the value zero.

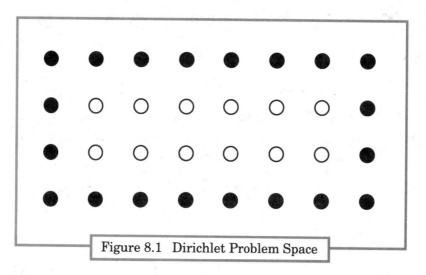

Figure 8.1   Dirichlet Problem Space

The neighbors of a cell are those whose coordinates differ by at most one. The state of a cell varies over time and successive states are related by the following *transition function*:

- Boundary cells have constant states.

- At non-boundary cells, the state at time $t+1$ is the average of the neighboring states at time t.

Thus, as time progresses, the values of the cells converge to a solution to the Laplace equation $\nabla^2\Theta = 0$, with the original values of Θ on the boundary. Typically, transitions are applied repeatedly until some convergence criterion is reached; for simplicity, the solution presented here will use a fixed number of transitions. The basic solution for the problem is a direct encoding of the transition function as outlined in Program 8.1.

For each i,j where $0 \leq i < x$, $0 \leq j < y$
    initialize $s_{i,j}$
    For each time t,
        if (not_on_boundary(i,j))
$$s_{i,j}^{t+1} = (s_{i-1,j}^{t} + s_{i+1,j}^{t} + s_{i,j-1}^{t} + s_{i,j+1}^{t})/4$$

Program 8.1 Abstract Formulation

8.2 Partitioning

Recall, from Section 7.1, that the central idea in partitioning is to divide the problem into logical entities that can be executed in parallel. Like most regular grid problems the Dirichlet problem can be partitioned using *domain decomposition*. This involves dividing the data domain of the program, in this case the grid, into segments that can be computed concurrently. There are only three reasonable divisions of the Dirichlet grid: by row, by column or by patches. The simple, by column partitioning shown in Figure 8.2 is used here.

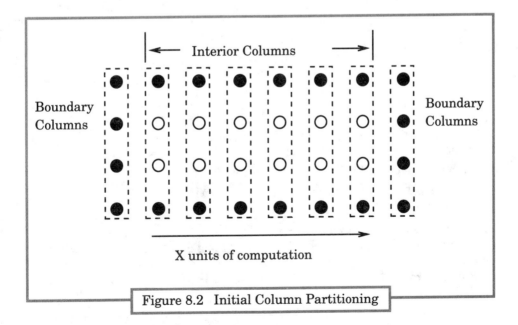

Figure 8.2 Initial Column Partitioning

> **Partitioning Refinement:** Begin with an abstract speci-
> fication of the problem, decide upon an initial partitioning
> strategy and refine the specification into an outline program
> incorporating the partitioning.

There are two types of calculation in this partitioning, corresponding to
boundary and *interior* columns. Program 8.2 outlines how the partitioning
can be specified as a *composition* of programs that compute these calculations.
The grid is composed of the first boundary column and a collection of other
columns that may execute in parallel (1). The other columns correspond to
either the final boundary (3) or an interior column with a collection of other
columns (2).

```
grid(...) {||  boundary(...), columns(...) }        /* 1 */

columns(...)
{ ?   interior  ->                                  /* 2 */
           {||   column(...), columns(...) },
      not_interior  ->                               /* 3 */
           boundary(...)
}
```

Program 8.2 Outline of Partitioning

The original problem solution, Program 8.1, can now be refined to use the
column partitioning by applying the transition function to *entire columns*.
This organization requires that each column calculation repeatedly execute
the following steps:

1. Send a copy of the column state to neighbors.
2. Receive a copy of the state of each neighboring column.
3. Apply the transition function to all cells in the column.

The send and receive actions at Steps 1 and 2 explicitly encode the data dependencies in Program 8.1. Synchronization is achieved by virtue of Step 2:
no column calculation may execute Step 3 until all of the required input is
received. Program 8.3 shows the complete partitioning and interior column
calculations.

Three *streams*, represented by definition variables, are used to implement
the necessary communication: Two (Li,Ri) are used to receive neighboring

```
/* grid(t_iterations,x_units) */

grid(t,x) {|| boundary(t,l,O), columns(t,x−1,O,l) }          /* 1 */

columns(t,x,Li,O)
{ ?  x > 1 −>
            {|| column(t,Li,O,Ri), columns(t,x-1,O,Ri) },     /* 2 */
      x == 1 −>
            boundary(t,Li,O)                                  /* 3 */
}

column(t,Li,O,Ri)                                             /* 4 */
{|| initialize(s), column1(t,s,Li,O,Ri) }

column1(t,s,Li,O,Ri)
{|| O=[s | O1],                                               /* 5 */
    t > 0, Li ? = [L | Li1], Ri ? = [R | Ri1] −>             /* 6 */
            {|| transition(s,L,R,s1),                         /* 7 */
                column1(t−1,s1,Li1,O1,Ri1)                    /* 8 */
            }
}
```

Program 8.3 Partitioning and Interior Column Refinements

columns, the other (O) is used to send the current state to *both* neighbors. Figure 8.3 shows how the streams are connected via the recursive call to columns (2): The right input and output of one column are connected to the left output and input of the next column.

Initially, the column state s is created and the transition function is repeatedly applied by column1 in Program 8.3. On each iteration, the state s is sent to *both* neighboring columns using a single definition statement (5), columns are received from neighbors using matching (6), the transition function is executed to produce a new state s1 (7) and the program continues with one less time step remaining (8). A program similar to the column calculation may be used for boundary calculations; it uses only a single input and output stream.

The program progresses toward termination by virtue of the metric t. Initially, the expected value of t is some positive integer. At each iteration of the column1 program, t is decremented (8). Eventually, t reaches the value zero and the program terminates since the test t > 0 is not satisfied (6).

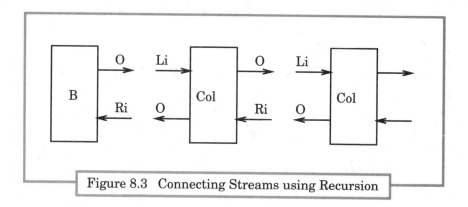

Figure 8.3   Connecting Streams using Recursion

The program defined thus far has used parallel composition extensively. There are two notable aspects to the composition used:

- Unless otherwise specified, all programs composed in parallel execute at the *same computer*. Parallel composition signifies how a program *may* be divided into concurrent components but does not indicate how these components will be executed.

- All arguments to programs composed in parallel are definitions. Thus, a program will operate in the same manner irrespective of *where* within a parallel machine it is executed.

8.3   Mapping

Having expressed a partitioning, the program can now be refined to include a *mapping*; this mapping expresses *where* the concurrent partitions are to execute within a parallel machine. For reasons of portability, we express mappings with respect to a generic *virtual machine* rather than a specific architecture.

A virtual machine is simply a convenient programming structure such as a *ring, mesh* or *tree*. These structures are embedded in the physical structure of a given machine via appropriate compiler tools. Thus the task of mapping is reduced to a simpler task of finding an appropriate computational structure. For example, a partitioning of the Dirichlet problem based on patches of the data domain would map directly to a mesh. Since we have chosen a partitioning based on column division, a ring mapping is more convenient.

> **Mapping Refinement:** Refine the partitioning to include
> mapping constructs that cause partitions to be allocated to
> computers.

Recall from Section 8.2 that all programs are executed within the same
computer unless otherwise specified. To indicate where a program should be
executed, we will annotate a program call with the location of a computer. For
example:

$$p(\ldots) \{ ||\ f(\ldots), g(\ldots) @ position, h(\ldots)\ \}$$

This composition states that programs f and h execute at the same computer
as program p, while program g executes at some other position within a virtual
machine. The values used in the position specification depend on the type of
virtual machine to be used. We will use two virtual machines: a ring and an
enumerated machine. The ring allows programs to be executed at forward or
backward relative positions using the notation @fwd or @bwd. The enumerated machine assigns n virtual computers a numerical order from zero to $n-1$;
each computer is referenced numerically using the notation @n.

Program 8.4 is a refinement of Program 8.2 that maps the column partitioning to a ring virtual machine. The only changes to the original program
are the addition of the two @fwd annotations (1,2). The program recursively
unwinds over a ring: At each step, a column program is executed at the current computer and the recursive call to columns carries the program forward
around the ring (2).

```
grid(...) {||  boundary(...), columns(...)@fwd }          /* 1 */

columns(...)
{ ?   interior ->
            {||   column(...), columns(...)@fwd },         /* 2 */
       not_interior ->
            boundary(...)
}
```

Program 8.4 Ring Mapping Refinement

Program 8.5 shows an alternative mapping using enumeration. In this
program all iterations of the columns program execute in a single computer;

column programs are distributed to computers in numeric sequence. The definition variable C is used to specify the number of the next computer to receive a column; L indicates the last computer to receive a column. Variables used in mappings are quoted, as in ′C, to distinguish them from predefined mappings such as fwd.

```
grid(...L) {|| boundary(...)@0, columns(...1,L) }        /* 1 */

columns(...C,L)
{ ?   C < L ->                                           /* 2 */
          {||   column(...)@′C, columns(...C+1,L) },
      C == L ->                                          /* 3 */
          boundary(...)@′L
}
```

Program 8.5 Enumerated Mapping Refinement

Recursive Mapping: Recursion is used to unwind a program across a parallel machine.

Programs 8.4 and 8.5 both use the same basic partitioning. The mapping is added as a refinement of Program 8.2 which defined this partitioning; thus it is possible to reason about the mapping independently and to experiment with alternatives. The resulting programs are *scalable*: Allocating more computers does not affect their definition. Moreover, provided that the same virtual machines are supported on a variety of parallel architectures, the programs are *portable*.

Recall, from Section 7.1, that a primary goal in parallel programming is to *hide latency with computation*. In Programs 8.4 and 8.5 this is achieved through parallel composition. Two program components that execute in parallel may utilize the *same* computer; one may be inoperative while waiting for communication but the other may nevertheless continue with useful work.

8.4   Granularity Control

Recall, from Section 7.2, that the granularity of a computation is the ratio of computation to communication. For example, in the solution we have adopted to the Dirichlet problem, four messages, each having the length of a single column, are required to calculate a single column of the new state. Let us consider an alternative partitioning of the problem that uses *interior subgrids* rather than columns as illustrated in Figure 8.4. The program to implement this partitioning is *precisely* that used in Program 8.3. Only the unit of computation has changed, not the basic partitioning. The definition of the unit of computation is embedded in the transition program; this program alone need be modified to communicate and operate on a subgrid rather than a column.

Granularity Refinement: Look for methods to group operations on the same data and refine the program by parameterizing grain size.

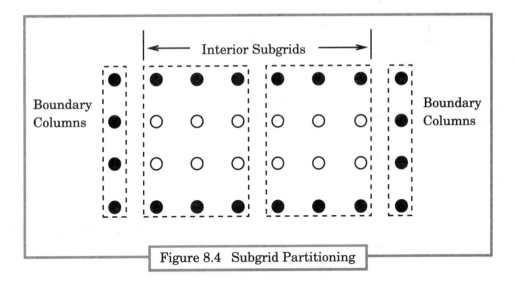

Figure 8.4   Subgrid Partitioning

Unfortunately, if the unit of computation is an entire subgrid, then Program 8.3 communicates some data that is irrelevant: Only columns on the edge of a subgrid are needed to compute neighboring subgrids. However, Program 8.3 can be refined to communicate only the necessary subgrid edges. To achieve this organization, a program get_edge is defined that retrieves a left or right edge from a subgrid; its first argument indicates which edge to retrieve (0=left, 1=right). Program 8.6 shows a refinement of Program 8.3 that uses the get_edge program. Unlike Program 8.3, this program uses two distinct output streams per subgrid since the information sent to neighbors is now different.

```
grid(t,x) {||  boundary(t,I,O), columns(t,x–1,O,I) }              /* 1 */

columns(t,x,Li,Lo)
{ ?   x > 1 ->
            {||   column(t,Li,Lo,Ri,Ro), columns(t,x-1,Ro,Ri) },  /* 2 */
      x == 1 ->
            boundary(t,Li,Lo)                                     /* 3 */
}

column(t,Li,Lo,Ri,Ro)                                             /* 4 */
{||   initialize(s), column1(t,s,Li,Lo,Ri,Ro) }

column1(t,s,Li,Lo,Ri,Ro)
{||   get_edge(0,s,LE), get_edge(1,s,RE),
      Lo=[LE | Lo1], Ro=[RE | Ro1],
      t > 0, Li ?= [L | Li1], Ri ?= [R | Ri1] ->
            {||   transition(s,L,R,s1),
                  column1(t–1,s1,Li1,Lo1,Ri1,Ro1)
            }
}
```

Program 8.6   Granularity Refinement

Program 8.6 sends four messages, each the size of a single column, to compute an entire subgrid computation. The length of the subgrid (x) may alter without affecting the quantity of communication; thus the ratio of communication to computation is completely under the programmer's control.

8.5   Memory Management

All of the programs presented in previous sections have employed only parallel and choice compositions with definition variables. Complete parallel programs can be generated with just these three ideas; it is strongly recommended that all program development be initially conducted in this manner. The programs that result typically copy data rather than update data structures. For example, consider the transition program used in Program 8.3. This takes as arguments a state s, neighboring left and right columns (L and R) and produces a new state s1. If implemented using only definitions, copying would be required to achieve this functionality: state s is a definition and thus can be defined only once. It is clear that s will not be used after s1 is computed; moreover, the computation of a single column will reside in a single computer under both mapping schemes. Thus it is preferable to reuse the memory for s to represent the new state s1.

To express the concept of memory reuse, *mutable variables* are used in subsequent program refinements. Recall, from Section 6.1, that these variables correspond exactly to variables that appear in conventional languages such as C and Fortran: integers (int), double precision floating-point numbers (double), characters (char) and one-dimensional arrays of these types.

Unfortunately, it is not sufficient to allow a program to update the state s in the transition program example. It is also necessary to guarantee that no other program, running concurrently, accesses the variable while it is in some partial state. To achieve this we use two ideas:

1. Recall, from Section 8.2, that all arguments to programs composed in parallel are definitions. Thus parallel program components do not share mutable variables; our program obeys Design Rule 1 in Section 6.4.

2. Programs that share mutable variables may be composed *sequentially*.

Program 8.7 is a refinement of Program 8.3 that adds memory optimization to update the state s in place. A declaration is used to create a double precision floating-point array s of size YMAX (1); we assume for simplicity that YMAX is a constant. The array s represents the state of a column in the grid and is passed as a parameter to other programs (2). Sequential composition is used to control the sequence of accesses to state s (3).

Recall Design Rule 2 in Section 6.4: When used in definitions, mutable variables are *snapshot* or copied. Thus, the single definition O=[s | O1] sends a copy of the state s to both neighboring columns (4). The state s is updated using an *assignment* operation (:=) taken from conventional languages; thus it need not be copied (5).

Memory Refinement: Refine the program by adding mutable variables and sequential composition to control updates to important data structures.

Notice that all of the arguments to the column program are definitions, and thus it may still be combined with other programs using parallel composition even though it modifies memory. None of the partitioning, mapping or granularity refinements are affected by this optimization.

```
column(t,Li,O,Ri)
double s[YMAX];                                    /* 1 */
{ ;   initialize(s), column1(t,s,Li,O,Ri) }        /* 2,3 */

column1(t,s,Li,O,Ri)
double s[];                                        /* 2 */
{ ;   O=[s | O1],                                  /* 3,4 */
      t > 0, Li ? = [L | Li1], Ri ? = [R | Ri1]  ->
            { ;   transition(1,YMAX–1,s,L,R,s[0]),  /* 3 */
                  column1(t–1,s,Li1,O1,Ri1)
            }
}

transition(n,y,s,L,R,tmp1)
double s[];                                        /* 2 */
      n < y  ->
            { ;   tmp=s[n],                         /* 3 */
                  s[n]  := (tmp1+s[n+1]+L[n]+R[n])/4,  /* 5 */
                  transition(n+1,y,s,L,R,tmp)      /* 2 */
            }
```

Program 8.7 Memory Optimization Refinement

8.6   Code Reuse

It is likely that the basic transition function used in this problem exists in a mathematical library or an existing program written in C or Fortran. Alternatively, we may desire the use of one of these languages for improved, machine-specific performance of sequential code. Since the basic idea in programming is to combine programs, the language in which these programs are expressed is not particularly important: Any program can be exchanged for an equivalent program expressed in some other language. For example, it is possible to replace PCN programs, using definitions, by C or Fortran programs, provided the following constraints are met:

- C and Fortran programs are executed as an atomic unit and begin execution only when all definition variables used as parameters are defined.

- All arguments are passed by reference and output is generated via mutable variables declared in PCN.

For example, the transition program expressed using sequential composition in Program 8.7 can be expressed in Fortran as shown in Program 8.8.

```
        SUBROUTINE TRANSITION(N1,Y,S,L,R,TMP1)
        DOUBLE PRECISION S(0:Y), L(0:Y), R(0:Y)
        INTEGER N,N1,Y,TMP1
        DO 50 N=N1,Y
            TMP=S[N]
            S[N]=(TMP1+S(N+1)+L(N)+R(N))/4
            TMP1=TMP
   50   CONTINUE
        RETURN
        END
```

Program 8.8 Fortran Refinement

To use Program 8.8 as part of Program 8.7, the PCN transition program is simply omitted and replaced by a compiler directive of the form

-foreign("file1", "file2", ...)

This directive informs the compiler where to find object code or libraries that implement any omitted programs. For example, if Program 8.8 were placed in a file *transition.f* and compiled with the Unix command "f77 -c transition.f", an object file *transition.o* will be generated. The following directive could then be added to Program 8.7.

-foreign("transition.o")

Notice, once again, that this code replacement does not affect any of the earlier refinements; it simply exchanges a sequential PCN program for a faster machine-specific equivalent.

The final solution for the Dirichlet problem is shown in Program 8.9.

8.7   Communication Protocols

The programs presented in this chapter have all used a single programming technique for expressing communication and synchronization. Let us briefly review this technique in a more general setting. The central protocol used in the Dirichlet problem is that of a producer and a set of associated consumers: Each column produces a value and sends it to all neighboring columns; these then consume the value and compute the next state of the computation.

```
/* grid.a: transition.o, initialize.o, binitialize.o get_edge.o */

-foreign("grid.a")

/* grid(TimeSteps,Xsubgrids,Ycells,GridWidth) */

grid(t,x,y,GW)
{|| boundary(t,y,I,O), columns(t,x−1,y,GW,O,I)@fwd }

columns(t,x,y,GW,Li,Lo)
{ ?  x > 1 −>
            {||   column(t,y,GW,y*GW,Li,Lo,Ri,Ro),
                  columns(t,x-1,y,GW,Ro,Ri)@fwd
            },
      x == 1 −> boundary(t,y,Li,Lo)
}

column(t,y,GW,GS,Li,Lo,Ri,Ro)
double s[GS], e[y];
{ ;   initialize(y,GW,s), column1(t,y,GW,s,e,Li,Lo,Ri,Ro) }

column1(t,y,GW,s,e,Li,Lo,Ri,Ro)
double s[], e[];
{ ;   get_edge(0,s,e), Lo=[e | Lo1],
      get_edge(1,s,e), Ro=[e | Ro1],
      t > 0, Li ?= [L1 | Li1], Ri ?= [R1 | Ri1] −>
            { ;   transition(y,GW,s,L1,R1),
                  column1(t−1,y,GW,s,e,Li1,Lo1,Ri1,Ro1)
            }
}

boundary(t,y,Bi,Bo)
double s[y];
{ ;   binitialize(y,s), Bo=[s | Bo1], boundary1(t,s,Bi,Bo1) }

boundary1(t,s,Bi,Bo)
double s[];
t > 0, Bi ?= [_ | Bi1] −>
      { ; Bo=[s | Bo1], boundary1(t−1,s,Bi1,Bo1) }
```

Program 8.9 Final Dirichlet Problem Solution

8.7.1 Producer-Consumers

The general form of the *producer-consumers* protocol is shown in Figure 8.5; messages originate at a producer program and are received by some number of consumers.

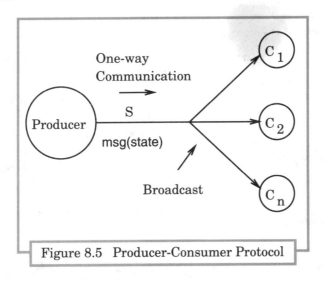

Figure 8.5   Producer-Consumer Protocol

Program 8.10 is a generic implementation of this protocol that illustrates communication and synchronization. It assumes that initially the producer and consumers share a single definition variable, for example

$\{| |$ producer(10,S), consumer$_1$(S), consumer$_2$(S), ... consumer$_n$(S) $\}$

The producer uses a definition statement similar to S=[msg(state) | S1] to send a single message to all consumers. This message may include a copy of the producer's local state (1). The producer then updates the state (2) and recursively sends more messages (3). Notice that although S is defined only once, many messages are sent to each consumer.

Each consumer synchronizes using a pattern match S?=[msg(state) | S1] (5). If the producer has not yet produced a message, this will cause the consumer to wait. When a message arrives, the consumer uses it and recursively accepts more messages (6). Eventually, the producer terminates (4) and ends transmission (S=[ ]). This allows the consumer to terminate.

In this protocol there is nothing to prevent the producer from running ahead of the consumer and creating a large number of messages. If this were to happen, the underlying implementation of the protocol must save any messages that have not been consumed until the consumer eventually executes.

```
producer(n,S) double state[SIZE]; produce(n,S,state)

produce(n,S,state)
double state[ ];
{ ?  n > 0 ->
            { ;   S=[msg(state) | S1],              /* 1 */
                  update(state),                    /* 2 */
                  produce(n-1,S1,state)             /* 3 */
            },
        n == 0  -> S=[]                             /* 4 */
}


consumer(S)
S ?= [msg(state) | S1] ->                           /* 5 */
     {||   use(state), consumer(S1) }               /* 6 */
```

Program 8.10 Producer-Consumers Protocol

Typically, however, this message buffering does not occur in practice since problems inherently place limits on message sending. For example, in the Dirichlet problem the synchronization of the algorithm forces the number of outstanding messages to be at most one. Recall that the basic iterative scheme repeatedly sends a message, receives a message and then computes. All messages sent must be received before the next compute stage and thus before the next sending cycle. Thus, at most one message is outstanding due to the *algorithm*, even though the protocol allows unbounded communication.

> **Producer-Consumers:** One-way unbounded communication protocol.

8.7.2 Bounded Buffer

Rare situations do occur in which there is no inherent limit on the number of outstanding messages. In these cases, a simple reorganization of the producer-consumers protocol can be used to place a fixed limit on the number of outstanding messages. The generic organization of this technique, termed the *bounded buffer*, is shown in Program 8.11.

```
producer(n,B) double state[SIZE]; produce(n,B,state)

produce(n,B,state)
double state[ ];
{ ?   n > 0, B?=[Slot | B1] ->                        /* 1 */
          { ;   Slot=msg(state),                      /* 2 */
                update(state),                        /* 3 */
                produce(n-1,B1,state)                 /* 4 */
          },
      n == 0, S?=[Slot | _] -> Slot=["done"]          /* 5 */
}

consumer(Bb,Be)
Bb ? = [msg(state) | Bm] ->                           /* 6 */
      {| |   use(state),                              /* 7 */
            Be=[NewSlot | Be1]                        /* 8 */
            consumer(Bm,Be1)                          /* 9 */
      }
```

Program 8.11 Bounded-Buffer Protocol

The producer and consumer share a common buffer that initially contains some fixed number of message *slots* represented by definition variables. For example, the following composition involves a producer and consumer that share a four-element buffer:

{| | Buffer=[S1,S2,S3 | End], producer(10,Buffer), consumer(Buffer,End) }

The producer waits until there is space in the buffer (1) and then sends a message to the consumer by placing it into the buffer (2). It continues producing until some termination condition is satisfied and then terminates transmission by placing a done message into the buffer (5). The consumer takes messages from the beginning of the buffer (6), uses them in some way (7), adds space to the end of the buffer (8), and recursively accepts other messages (9). The maximum number of messages that can be produced before the producer is forced to wait corresponds to the number of slots in the initial buffer.

> **Bounded-Buffer:** Provides a fixed upper bound on the number of messages that are sent but not received.

8.8 Summary

This chapter took a simple grid problem and demonstrated its solution through stepwise refinement. The design has emphasised a gradual development of the program from its initial specification. New refinement steps consider problems unique to parallel programming: partitioning, mapping, granularity control and memory management. At each refinement step, the program remains relatively intact and does not require extensive rewriting. Thus these stages of program development can be considered carefully and methodically, largely independent of one another.

Concurrent programs can be developed using only parallel composition, choice composition and definition variables. Sequential composition and mutable variables may be used purely for optimization after a suitable parallel program has been obtained. Since the unit of composition is a program, libraries of existing algorithms and mathematics can be reused within new parallel programs.

Finally, we have isolated two generic programming techniques that repeatedly occur in programming: the *producer-consumer* and *bounded-buffer* protocols. As we progress we will see that there are a small number of basic techniques. Parallel programming using definition variables is, in essence, the repeated use of these techniques in different guises.

Exercises

1. Modify the Dirichlet problem so that following every iteration the upper and lower y boundaries are exchanged.

2. Modify the Dirichlet problem so that following every iteration the upper and lower x boundaries are exchanged. Why is this more difficult than exchanging the y boundaries?

3. Modify the Dirichlet problem so that in the x direction *two* adjacent cells in each direction are used in the calculation of a cell.

4. Modify the Dirichlet problem to print the minimum cell value after every ten iterations.

5. Modify the Dirichlet problem to subtract the maximum cell value from all boundary cells at every third iteration.

6. Modify the Dirichlet problem to use a two-dimensional decomposition and map this decomposition to a ring virtual machine.

7. Modify the Dirichlet problem to use a two-dimensional decomposition and map this decomposition to an enumerated virtual machine.

8. Modify your solution to Question 6 to use a mesh virtual machine where allowable mapping annotations are north, east, south and west. What is the benefit of this mapping?

9. Generalize the Dirichlet problem to three dimensions but decompose the problem in only one dimension and map it to a ring.

10. Modify the Dirichlet problem to use a red-black (or checkerboard) iteration scheme. In this scheme every cell has a color: red or black. All of the neighbors of a given cell have the opposite color. Cells on the boundary have constant values. At each step in the iteration process either the red or black points are updated: red values are updated using black values and vice-versa.

11. Modify your solution to Question 10 to subtract the minimum black value from every red point after every tenth iteration.

12. Write a program that generates all the integers from 20 to 1000 in increments of 10 and another that sums these numbers and prints the result.

13. Modify the program in Question 12 to ensure that at most five numbers exist at one time.

14. Given a C program that generates a random number, sum 100 random numbers.

15. Write a producer-consumer protocol that does not use mutable state.

16. Write a program ring that generates a set of programs connected in a ring. One program should generate the alphabet, one character at a time, and send it to the right. The alphabet should rotate around the ring ten times and, on arriving at the origin, the program should terminate.

17. Write a producer-consumer protocol where each program sends and receives three messages at a time.

18. Write a generic bounded-buffer program in which the consumer terminates message transmission.

19. Write a program called filter that accepts a stream of integers and generates an output stream of integers. The output contains all of the input integers except the number 2; all 2's are counted and the number of 2's that occur in the input is printed when the filter terminates.

20. Write a program scatter that accepts an input stream and generates ten output streams. It receives messages of the form {N,M} where N is a number between 0 and 10. For each message on the input stream the scatter program places message M on the first N output streams.

21. Write two programs expand and contract. The expand program takes a single cell state and generates some number of duplicate cell states. The contract program takes some number of cell states and generates a single cell state by averaging.

    Using these programs, write a version of the Dirichlet problem that expands and contracts the grid as the program executes. You should work on a given grid for a specified number of iterations before expanding or contracting the number of points. Initially your program should begin with a large number of points; it should then contract the grid size three times and then expand the grid three times.

CHAPTER

9

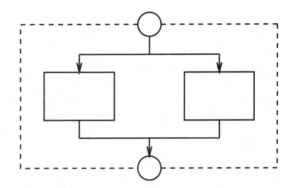

An Unstructured Grid Problem

> **Goals for this Chapter:**
>
> At the end of this chapter you should appreciate a variety
> of methods for organizing communication protocols. You
> should also understand how to detect termination condi-
> tions and be able to implement arbitrary testing predi-
> cates.

This chapter examines a simple unstructured grid problem. The problem
serves to demonstrate a variety of techniques for organizing communication
protocols and detecting termination criteria. The program design has been
carried out using stepwise refinement as presented in Chapter 8. However, in
order to focus on communication, we will not present a number of intermediate
refinement steps.

9.1 The Problem

The basic phenomena of fluid dynamics are diffusion and advection. Diffusion
involves the propagation of information in all directions from each point in
the computational domain. We have already seen this concept in the Dirichlet

example: The data at each point affects each point of its surroundings equally. Advection involves the propagation of information in a particular direction.

A familiar one-dimensional example of advection is provided by traffic flow on a highway. If we let t be a measure of time and x a measure of distance along the highway, then we define a *density* function $\rho(x,t)$ that signifies the number of cars per unit distance at position x and time t. We also define a *velocity* function $v(x,t)$ that signifies the average velocity of cars at position x and time t.

Consider a simple case where every car has the same velocity. Figure 9.1 shows how traffic moves along the highway in this case. The left curve shows the density of traffic at time t=0 and the right curve shows the density after some time dt. Every car has moved a distance vdt, thus the whole curve simply moves to the right by that distance.

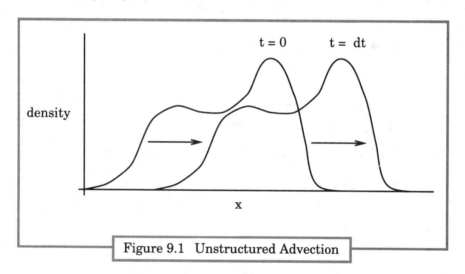

Figure 9.1   Unstructured Advection

To simulate traffic flow, suppose that there are *markers* at random places along the highway and that we know the density of cars in the *cells* between the markers. Figure 9.2 shows how the traffic is advected. At the top of the picture is the density field at time t=0. The area of the rectangle in a cell represents the number of cars in that cell. For each marker, we evaluate the density difference, or *flux*, between adjacent cells. We then create a rectangle whose height is the flux value and whose length is the propagation distance vdt. By simply adding all of the density differences in each cell to the original density field, the field is advected as shown at the bottom of Figure 9.2.

This form of advection can be simulated by a simple parallel algorithm outlined in Program 9.1. Each step of the algorithm consists of two phases. In Phase 1, the flux between neighboring cells is calculated. In Phase 2, flux is

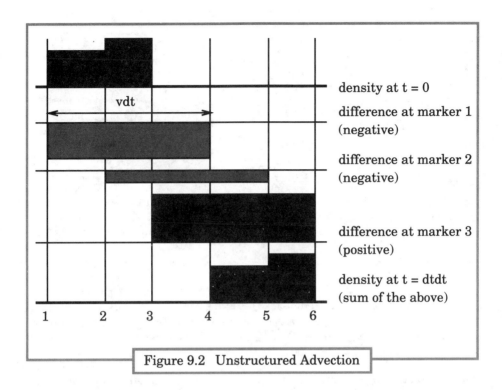

Figure 9.2 Unstructured Advection

For each cell i, where $0 \leq i < x$
    initialize cell state s_i
    For each time t,
        Phase 1: *flux calculation*
            $\text{flux}_i = \text{difference}(s_i^t, s_{i-1}^t)$
        Phase 2: *flux propagation*
            $s_i^{t+dt} = s_i^t + \sum_j \text{flux}_j$
            where $0 \leq j < x$ and $i - vdt < j \leq i$

Program 9.1 Abstract Formulation

propagated downstream from cell to cell for a distance of vdt. The flux is used to *update* the density of each cell through which it passes. Figure 9.3 shows how information propagates using this algorithm: Arrows denote the flow of information, the lengths of the arrows signify the area of the grid where the information is relevant, and labels on the arrows signify which phase of the algorithm is concerned.

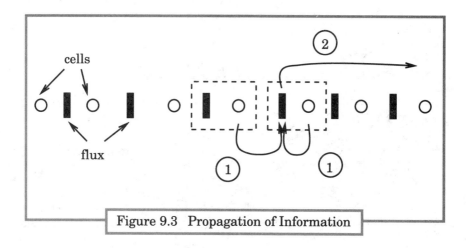

Figure 9.3   Propagation of Information

To implement the algorithm it is convenient to associate flux with the cell to its right as shown by the dotted boxes in Figure 9.3. In addition, we associate the calculated flux with the value vdt to form a flux rectangle; this rectangle is communicated downstream. In this manner, it is possible for a cell to decide locally if it is affected by a given flux value.

The algorithm as specified involves a subtle synchronization problem that results from the propagation of information. Consider a single iteration of cell i at time t: To calculate s_i^{t+dt}, the state of a neighboring cell at time t, s_{i-1}^t, must be available. However, since all cells execute the same algorithm, the neighboring cell must have completed Phase 2 so that its state is completely updated. To complete Phase 2, a given cell must be able to detect the termination criterion: *all updates have been performed.* Since the number of updates a cell performs is dependent on its distance from other cells, it is not possible to determine *a priori* how many updates a given cell is required to perform at each iteration.

To overcome this problem we use an alternative termination criterion: *all rectangles have propagated to completion.* From this criterion it follows that all updates on every cell are complete. The new termination criterion involves two separate activities:

1. Local Termination: Detecting when a single rectangle has propagated to completion.

2. Global Termination: Detecting that all rectangles have completed propagation and thus the next iteration has begun.

We begin the program design by neglecting these activities and focusing on the basic flow of information. Subsequently, we add refinement steps to implement each of these activities and thus solve the synchronization problem.

9.2 Partitioning and Mapping

The program design is initiated by choosing a unit of computation that affords maximal concurrency and scalability: This corresponds to a single cell in the domain. Program 9.2 is an initial refinement of the program that uses *domain decomposition* to partition the grid, containing m cells, into n parts. Each part contains $c = m/n$ cells and is mapped to a different computer; for simplicity we assume m is a multiple of n. Each part of the domain is subsequently divided into c equal segments; one cell is placed at a random location within each segment.

```
grid(n,c,...) {|| parts(n,c,R,...), high(R) }        /* 1 */

parts(n,c,R,...)
{ ?n > 0 ->                                           /* 2 */
        {|| parts(n–1,c,L,...)@bwd,
            part(n,c,L,R,...)
        },
     default -> low(R,...)                            /* 3 */
}

part(n,c,L,R,...) cells(n,c,L,R,...)                  /* 4 */

cells(n,c,L,R,...)
{ ? c > 0 ->
        {|| cells(n,c–1,L,M,...),                     /* 5 */
            start_cell(n,c,M,R,...)                   /* 6 */
        },
     default -> R=L
}

start_cell(n,c,L,R,...)
double s[SMAX], fr[FRMAX];
{ ; random(n,c,position),                            /* 7 */
    init(position,s),                                 /* 8 */
    cell(s,fr,L,R,...)                                /* 9 */
}
```

Program 9.2 Partitioning and Mapping

An inspection of the data dependencies in Program 9.1 shows that information is propagated between adjacent cells as indicated by the arrows in Figure 9.3. To achieve this flow of information, each cell need only communicate with its right neighbor. Figure 9.4 shows how Program 9.2 constructs an initial connection between cells in the grid to allow this communication.

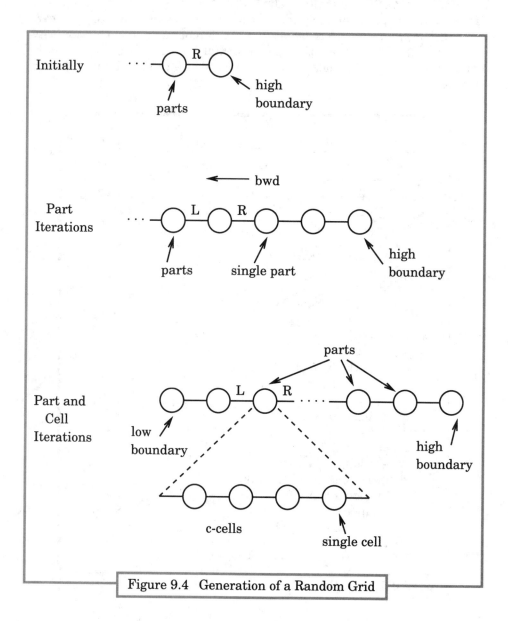

Figure 9.4   Generation of a Random Grid

Initially, the grid is composed of only a high boundary and a collection of n parts (1); the right end of the parts are connected to the high boundary (R). The parts are composed of either a low boundary (3) *or* a single part together with other parts that exist at computers behind the current computer (2). A single part consists of c cells (4). Each set of cells consists of $c - 1$ cells connected from the left of a part L to some middle point M (5); the final cell is connected between this middle point M and the right end of the part R (6).

A cell is placed at a random position in the grid on the interval (n, c) to $(n, c + 1)$ (7) and its state is initialized (8). Thus, Program 9.2 generates a collection of cells that are partitioned into n parts, one per computer. Each cell has two streams that allow it to communicate with its neighbors.

Continuing with the refinement, we now directly encode the actions of Program 9.1 for a single interior cell. Program 9.3 implements a single cell and performs the following operations at every iteration of the algorithm:

1. Send cell state s_i^t to the right (1).

2. Receive cell state s_{i-1}^t from the left (2).

3. Execute a difference program to obtain a flux rectangle (3).

4. Propagate the flux rectangle to the right (4).

5. Repeatedly receive flux rectangles and perform updates (5). If the cell is affected by a flux rectangle, then the cell density is updated using the received flux value and the flux rectangle is propagated to the right; otherwise, the flux rectangle is discarded.

```
cell(s,fr,L,R,...)
double s[ ],fr[ ];
{ ; R = [s | R1]                        /* 1 */
    L ?= [si | L1] ->                    /* 2 */
        { ; difference(s,si,fr),         /* 3 */
            R1 = [fr | R2],              /* 4 */
            updates(s,L1,L2,R2,R3,...),  /* 5 */
            cell(s,fr,L2,R3,...)         /* repeat */
        }
}
```

Program 9.3 Initial Cell Definition

9.3   Local Termination Refinement

Thus far the program has neglected the synchronization problem discussed in Section 9.1. In solving this problem we first focus on organizing communication so that a cell detects when its own flux rectangle has completely propagated. Figure 9.5 shows how this is achieved.

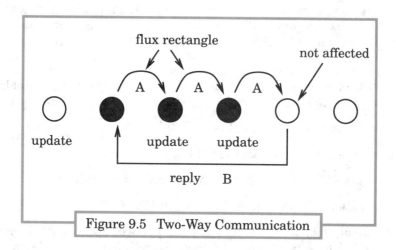

Figure 9.5   Two-Way Communication

A flux rectangle is propagated in a message that also contains an indication of where the message originated; this communication is indicated by the arrows marked A. If the rectangle enters a cell that is affected by it, an update operation is performed and the rectangle is propagated further. If the rectangle reaches a cell that is not affected by it, no further propagation is needed; in this case a message is sent to the originating cell to indicate that the rectangle has now completely propagated. This *reply* message is indicated by the arrow marked B in Figure 9.5.

To add this protocol to the program design we need only refine the operation of a single cell described by Program 9.3. This refinement is shown in Program 9.4. To propagate its flux rectangle, a cell builds a message containing a snapshot of the rectangle and a *slot* corresponding to a reply (1); the slot is represented by a definition variable d. When performing updates a cell continually receives messages from the left (3). If the cell is affected by the message, an update is performed and the message is propagated (4); otherwise, a reply message is generated (5). When a cell receives a reply, it detects that its own rectangle has completely propagated by defining the variable p (2).

```
cell(s,fr,L,R,...)
double s[ ],fr[ ];
{ ; R = [s | R1]
    L ? = [si | L1] ->
        { ; difference(s,si,fr),
            R1 = [{fr,d} | R2],                          /* 1 */
            {|| updates(s,L1,L2,R2,R3,...),
                data(d) -> p="done"                      /* 2 */
            },
            cell(s,fr,L2,R3,...)
        }
}

updates(s,Lb,Le,Rb,Re,...)
double s[ ]; int a;
Lb ? = [{fr,d} | Lm] ->                                  /* 3 */
    { ; affected_by(s,fr,a),
        { ? a == 1 -> { ; update(s,fr), Rb=[{fr,d} | Rm] },   /* 4 */
            default -> {|| d="reply", Rb=Rm }            /* 5 */
        },
        updates(s,Lm,Le,Rm,Re,...),
    }
```

Program 9.4 State Propagation Refinement

Two-way Communication: A producer sends a message
containing a *slot* corresponding to a reply; it then waits for
the reply to be defined. The consumer defines the slot causing
a reply to be sent.

Notice that the updates program, as currently defined, never terminates.
Recall from Section 9.1 that it is not possible for a cell to determine *a priori*
when all messages have arrived. Thus, the *updates* program may not terminate until it is known that a single iteration of the simulation is complete.
This requires that the criterion *all rectangles have completed propagation* be
detected; we now turn to the problem of detecting this situation.

9.4 Global Termination Refinement

In order to detect that all rectangles have been propagated we use the programming technique shown in Figure 9.6(a). Every cell is linked into a communication chain that begins and ends at a detector program. Initially, a message is sent by the detector to the first cell in the chain. When a cell detects that its own rectangle has completely propagated, it forwards any messages appearing on its left to the cell at its right. Eventually, the original message appears back at the detector indicating that all cells have completely propagated their states. A message is then broadcast to all cells to notify them that the current iteration is complete, as shown in Figure 9.6(b).

Programs 9.5 and 9.6 refine Programs 9.2 and 9.4 to incorporate both the protocols shown in Figure 9.6. The grid is generated in the manner described in Section 9.2; flux rectangles are propagated as described in Section 9.3. In addition, a termination detection chain is threaded through all cells represented by the variables Lt, Mt and Rt. All cells receive a broadcast stream represented by the variable Gs.

> **Detecting Termination:** Chain programs together and place a constant on the left of the chain. When a program detects termination it closes a section of the chain. Eventually, the constant appears at the right end of the chain signifying termination.

When the program begins execution, a detector is executed that detects the global termination condition: *all flux rectangles have propagated* (1). The detector initially sends a done message to the leftmost cell via the variable Lt (2). Each cell forwards the done message when its own rectangle has completely propagated (7). When the detector receives a done message on the right side of the chain, it is assured that all rectangles have propagated (3); a go message is then issued on the broadcast stream Gs (4). This informs all cells to terminate processing updates (9) and begin the next iteration (8). Eventually, after t iterations, the detector terminates the computation by closing the global broadcast stream (6).

> **Global Broadcast:** A single producer generates a stream that is consumed by many consumers. Thus messages are broadcast to every consumer.

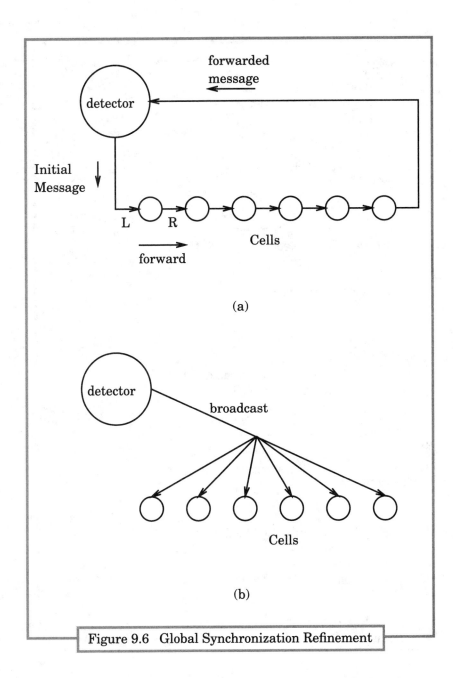

Figure 9.6   Global Synchronization Refinement

```
    grid(t,n,c)                                      /* 1 */
    {||  detector(t,Lt,Rt,Gs),
         parts(n,c,R,Lt,Rt,Gs),
         high(R)
    }

    detector(t,Lt,Rt,Gs)
    { ? t > 0 ->
            {||  Lt=["done" | Lt1],                  /* 2 */
                 Rt ? = ["done" | Rt1] ->            /* 3 */
                 {||  Gs=["go" | Gs1],               /* 4 */
                      detector(t–1,Lt1,Rt1,Gs1)      /* 5 */
                 }
            },
         t == 0 -> {|| Lt=[], Gs=[]}                 /* 6 */
    }

    parts(n,c,R,Lt,Rt,Gs)
    { ? n > 0 ->
            {||  parts(n–1,c,L,Lt,Mt,Gs)@bwd,
                 part(n,c,L,R,Mt,Rt,Gs)
            },
         default  -> {|| Rt=Lt, low(R,Gs) }
    }

    part(n,c,L,R,Lt,Rt,Gs) cells(n,c,L,R,Lt,Rt,Gs)

    cells(n,c,L,R,Lt,Rt,Gs)
    { ? c > 0 ->
            {||  cells(n,c–1,L,M,Lt,Mt,Gs),
                 start_cell(n,c,M,R,Mt,Rt,Gs)
            },
         default  -> {|| R=L, Rt=Lt }
    }
```

Program 9.5 Global Termination Refinement: Part 1

```
start_cell(n,c,L,R,Lt,Rt,Gs)
double s[SMAX],fr[FRMAX];
{ ; random(n,c,position),
    init(position,s),
    cell(s,L,R,Lt,Rt,Gs)
}

cell(s,fr,L,R,Lt,Rt,Gs)
double s[ ],fr[ ];
{ ; R = [s | R1]
    L ? = [si | L1] ->
        { ; difference(s,si,fr),
            R1 = [{fr,d} | R2],
            {|| updates(s,L1,L2,R2,R3,Gs),
                Lt ? = [t | Lt1], data(d) -> Rt=[t | Rt1]      /* 7 */
            },
            Gs ? = ["go" | Gs1] ->                            /* 8 */
                cell(s,fr,L2,R3,Lt1,Rt1,Gs1)
        }
}

updates(s,Lb,Le,Rb,Re,Gs)
double s[ ]; int a;
{ ? Lb  ? = [{fr,d} | Lm] ->
        { ; affected_by(s,fr,a),
            { ? a == 1 -> { ; update(s,fr), Rb=[{fr,d} | Rm] },
                default -> {|| d="reply", Rb=Rm }
            },
            updates(s,Lm,Le,Rm,Re,Gs),
        },
    Gs ? = ["go" | _] -> {|| Le=Lb, Rb=Re },                  /* 9 */
    Gs ? = [] -> skip( )
}
```

Program 9.6 Global Termination Refinement: Part 2

9.5 Improving Termination Detection

The initial solution shown in Programs 9.5 and 9.6 suffers from the unfortunate problem that the synchronization chain propagates through the cells in a linear sequence. This is not problematic for cells contained within a single computer. However, it is preferable to allow all computers to detect termination independently. To achieve this organization the basic termination criterion, *all rectangles have propagated*, is divided into two separate parts:

1. All rectangles originating within computer i have propagated, and thus computer i has terminated.

2. All computers have terminated.

Given these assertions, the original termination criterion follows directly. Figure 9.7 illustrates how these new termination criteria can be used.

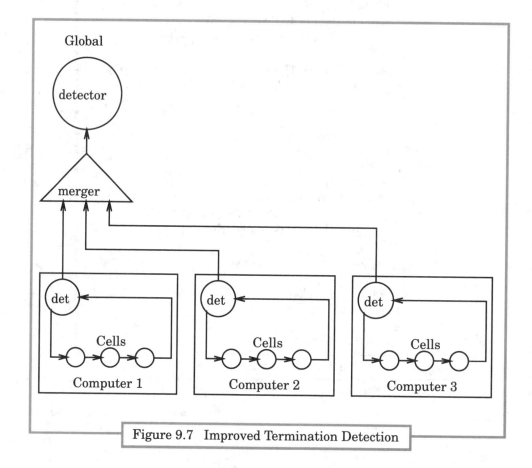

Figure 9.7   Improved Termination Detection

All cells within a single computer are associated with a detector and a synchronization chain similar to those used in Programs 9.5 and 9.6: Each detector signifies when Criterion 1 is satisfied by sending a message to a global detector. These messages are combined into a single stream. The global detector waits to receive n messages and then detects that all computers have terminated; thus the original criterion is satisfied and the global detector broadcasts a message to indicate that the current iteration is complete. This new organization requires the use of a *merger* program that is illustrated in Figure 9.8.

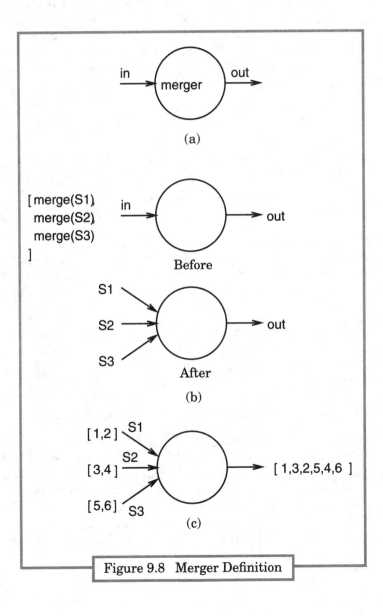

Figure 9.8   Merger Definition

Operationally, a merger is a program that takes n input streams and merges their contents into a single output stream. Initially, the merger has a single input stream and a single output stream as shown in Figure 9.8(a); usually, any messages appearing on the input are transferred directly to the output.

There is one special message of the form merge(S) which causes an additional input stream S to be added to the merger. Figure 9.8(b) shows how three streams are added to a single merger. Any messages appearing on the new input streams are interleaved into the output stream. Figure 9.8(c) illustrates the result of merging three streams and shows the output that occurs when messages are sent on each input. The only attribute of the merger that can be relied upon is that all messages appearing on the inputs eventually appear on the output.

> **Fair Merge:** Interleaves messages that appear on n input streams into a single output stream.

Programs 9.7 and 9.8 combine to form a refinement of Programs 9.5 and 9.6 with improved termination detection. The grid is generated in the usual manner but is associated with a global stepping program and an associated merger (1). As each part in the grid is generated it is connected into the merger via a new stream M (6).

The global stepper executes t iterations (2). During each iteration it waits for n messages to arrive, one from each computer (4); each message signifies that all cells within a computer have propagated their rectangles. The stepper then signifies that the next iteration is beginning by broadcasting a go message as in previous refinements of the program (5). After t iterations the stepper terminates and closes the broadcast stream allowing all cells to terminate (3).

Each collection of cells is associated with a detector and synchronization chain represented by the variables Lt and Rt (7). The detector uses the synchronization chain to detect that all cells within a computer have completed propagation of their states. This is achieved with the same technique used in Programs 9.5 and 9.6. Initially, a done message is placed on the left of the chain connecting all cells in a given computer (8). The detector waits to receive a done message on the right of this chain and then notifies the stepper that all cells within the computer have completed propagation (9). The remainder of the program is unchanged from previous refinements.

```
grid(t,n,c)
{|| stepper(n,t,Out,Gs), sys:merger(In,Out),                      /* 1 */
    parts(n,c,R,In,Gs), high(R)
}

stepper(n,t,In,Gs)
{ ? t > 0  -> {|| waitn(n,In,In1,Gs,Gs1), stepper(t-1,In1,Gs1) },   /* 2 */
    t == 0  -> Gs=[]                                                 /* 3 */
}

waitn(n,In,In1,Gs,Gs1)
{ ? n > 0, In ? = ["done" | In2]  -> waitn(n-1,In2,In1,Gs,Gs1),     /* 4 */
    n == 0  -> {|| In1=In, Gs=["go" | Gs1] }                        /* 5 */
}

parts(n,c,R,Ms,Gs)
{ ? n > 0 ->
        {|| Ms=[merge(M) | Ms1],                                    /* 6 */
            parts(n-1,c,L,Ms1,Gs)@bwd, part(n,c,L,R,M,Gs)
        },
    default -> {|| Ms=[], low(R,Gs) }
}

part(n,c,L,R,M,Gs) {|| detector(Lt,Rt,M), cells(n,c,L,R,Lt,Rt,Gs) }  /* 7 */

detector(Lt,Rt,M)
{|| Lt=["done" | Lt1],                                              /* 8 */
    Rt ? = ["done" | Rt1]  ->                                       /* 9 */
        {|| M=["done" | M1], detector(Lt1,Rt1,M1) }
}

cells(n,c,L,R,Lt,Rt,Gs)
{ ? c > 0 ->
        {|| cells(n,c-1,L,M,Lt,Mt,Gs), start_cell(n,c,M,R,Mt,Rt,Gs) },
    default -> {|| R=L, Rt=Lt }
}
```

Program 9.7 Improved Termination Detection: Part 1

```
#define SMAX 3
#define FRMAX 2
-foreign("cell.a")

start_cell(n,c,L,R,Lt,Rt,Gs)
double s[SMAX],fr[FRMAX];
{ ; random(n,c,position), init(position,s), cell(s,L,R,Lt,Rt,Gs) }

cell(s,fr,L,R,Lt,Rt,Gs)
double s[ ],fr[ ];
{ ; R = [s | R1]
    L ?= [si | L1] ->
        { ; difference(s,si,fr), R1 = [{fr,d} | R2],
            {|| updates(s,L1,L2,R2,R3,...),
                Lt ?= [t | Lt1], data(d) -> Rt=[t | Rt1]
            },
            Gs ?= ["go" | Gs1] -> cell(s,fr,L2,R3,Lt1,Rt1,Gs1)
        }
}

updates(s,Lb,Le,Rb,Re,Gs)
double s[ ]; int a;
{ ? Lb ?= [{fr,d} | Lm] ->
        { ; affected_by(s,fr,a),
            { ? a == 1 -> { ; update(s,fr), Rb=[{fr,d} | Rm] },
                default -> {|| d="reply", Rb=Rm }
            },
            updates(s,Lm,Le,Rm,Re,Gs),
        },
    Gs ?= ["go" | _] -> {|| Le=Lb, Rb=Re },
    Gs ?= [] -> skip( )
}

low(R,Gs) double s[SMAX]; { ; init(0,s), low1(s,R,Gs) }
low1(s,R,Gs) double s[ ];
    {|| R=[s | Rs], Gs ?= ["go" | Gs1] -> low1(s,Rs,Gs1) }

high(L) L ?= [{_,d} | Ls] -> {|| d="reply", high(Ls) }
```

Program 9.8 Improved Termination Detection: Part 2

9.6 Programming Techniques

In this chapter we have used a variety of programming techniques to implement complex communication protocols and termination criteria. Let us briefly pause to isolate these techniques and focus on their operation.

9.6.1 Broadcasting

Program 9.9 shows a generic code fragment that highlights the concept of broadcasting. A single producer program generates a single stream S of n messages (1). Some number of consumer programs all share the same stream (2). When the producer generates a message, all consumers receive the *same* message and use it. Thus the message is broadcast to all consumers.

```
program(n)
{|| producer(n,S),                                  /* 1 */
     consumer(S), consumer(S), consumer(S)          /* 2 */
}

producer(n,S)
{ ? n > 0 -> {|| S=["message" | S1], producer(n-1,S1) },
     n == 0 -> S=[]
}

consumer(S)
S ? = ["message" | S1] -> {|| use("message"), consumer(S1) }
```

Program 9.9 Generic Global Broadcasting

9.6.2 Two-Way Communication

Program 9.10 is a generic code fragment that highlights the ideas involved in two-way communication. Producer programs generate some number n of messages and expect replies; a consumer program receives messages from a variety of sources via a merger.

When a producer generates a message it adds a slot for a reply represented by a definition variable (1). It then waits for the variable to be defined and subsequently uses the reply value (2). When the consumer receives a message (3),

```
program(n)
{|| producer(n,S1), producer(n,S2), producer(n,S3),
    sys:merger([merge(S1),merge(S2), merge(S3)], Out),
    consumer(Out)
}

producer(n,S)
{ ? n > 0 ->
        {|| S=[message(reply) | S1],                    /* 1 */
            data(reply)  -> use(reply),                 /* 2 */
            producer(n–1,S1)
        },
      n == 0  -> S=[]
}

consumer(S)
S ? = [message(reply) | S1]  ->                          /* 3 */
     {|| reply="reply", consumer(S1) }                   /* 4 */
```

Program 9.10 Generic Two-Way Communication

it defines the reply variable (4) and thus causes a reply to be generated back to the appropriate producer. Notice that a consumer program need not know the identity of a producer in order to make a reply. This is implicit because each reply variable is generated by a single producer and received by at most one consumer.

9.6.3 Termination Detection

Program 9.11 is a generic code fragment for termination detection. A collection of n subprograms are linked together by a chain represented by the variables L, M and R; each time a new program is added to the chain, the chain is broken into subparts (3). The left of the chain is initially a constant (1). Subprograms perform some computation and eventually detect some termination criterion D; at this point a subprograms section of the chain is closed (4). Eventually, the original constant propagates from the left of the chain to the right and global termination can be detected (2).

Exactly the same technique can be used to define arbitrary testing predicates; these techniques are valuable because the guard of an implication may only contain simple predefined tests. Program 9.12 illustrates the technique

```
program(n)
{||  subprograms(n,"done",R),                        /* 1 */
     data(R) -> print("terminated")                  /* 2 */
}


subprograms(n,L,R)
{ ? n > 0 -> {|| subprogram(L,M), subprograms(M,R) }, /* 3 */
    n == 0 -> R=L
}

subprogram(L,R) {|| compute(D), data(D) -> R=L }      /* 4 */
```

Program 9.11 Generic Termination Detection

```
program(n)
{||  subprograms(n,"true",R),                        /* 1 */
     data(R) -> print(R)                             /* 2 */
}


subprograms(n,L,R)
{ ? n > 0 -> {|| subprogram(L,M), subprograms(M,R) },
    n == 0 -> R=L
}


subprogram(L,R)
{||  condition(Result),
     { ? Result == "true" -> R=L,                    /* 3 */
         Result == "false" -> R="false"              /* 4 */
     }
}
```

Program 9.12 Logical-And Implementation

and implements *logical-and*. Initially, the left of the chain is defined to be the constant true. Any subprogram that satisfies a particular condition simply closes its part of the chain (3). Any subprogram that falsifies the condition defines the right of the chain to be the constant false (4). Eventually, either true propagates throughout the chain and appears as the result, or false propagates from the rightmost falsifying program (2). This implements the logical-and of all the conditions.

9.7 Summary

In this chapter the *stream* concept developed in Chapter 8 has been used in a variety of alternative programming techniques. These include two-way communication, message broadcasting, termination detection, testing predicates and merging.

The design we have presented has shown only the most significant design steps. However, the basic progression is evident: Begin with a simple implementation, and incrementally remove bottlenecks and sequentiality through successive refinements.

Exercises

1. Refine Programs 9.7 and 9.8 to ensure that termination occurs.

2. In Program 9.4, updates are performed concurrently with detection that a rectangle has completely propagated. Why?

3. Assume that rectangles propagate at most a distance of five hops from their origin and simplify the program.

4. Modify Programs 9.7 and 9.8 to employ a spanning tree for detecting global termination rather than a merger.

5. Modify Programs 9.7 and 9.8 to operate on two-dimensional meshes.

6. Modify Programs 9.7 and 9.8 to operate on general graphs. You should describe the graph by a file containing numbered lines, e.g.,
   ```
   1   2   4
   3   4
   4   5
   5   6   7
   ```
   In this graph, node 1 is connected to nodes 2 and 4. Notice that arcs are only specified to *nodes of a higher number*.

7. Give a generic code fragment that implements logical-or.

8. Define a program integers(S,R) that returns true if all elements of the structure S are integers and false otherwise.

9. Define a program big(S,L,R) that returns true if any number contained in the structure S is greater than limit L and false otherwise.

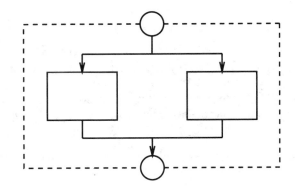

CHAPTER
10

An N-Body Simulation

Goals for this Chapter:

At the end of this chapter you should understand an alternative program design style based on the notion of *information hiding*. You should also understand how to construct search strategies with communicating programs, selectively distribute messages and create distributed data structures.

This chapter describes a simple two-dimensional, N-body simulation based on the Barnes-Hut algorithm. The problem serves to demonstrate a programming style based on the concept of *information hiding*. In this approach data structures and operations are associated and encapsulated within programs. The strategy allows central functional units to be isolated; the design process focuses on expressing program interactions. Programming techniques for search, message distribution and construction of distributed data structures will be considered within this framework. Although the N-body problem is interesting from a physics perspective, we will focus only on those aspects that serve to demonstrate programming concepts.

10.1 The Problem

Figure 10.1 shows a collection of n particles, or bodies, randomly scattered over a square, two-dimensional space. Each particle is described by an associated mass, position and velocity. Particles are subject to an applied force by virtue of other particles within the space. We are interested in algorithms for simulating the movement of the particles in time.

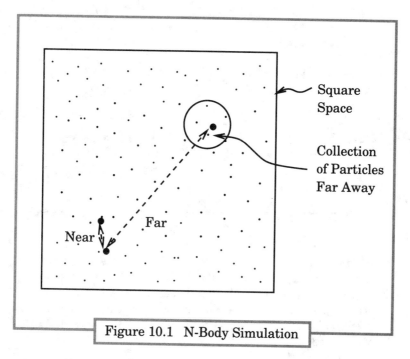

Figure 10.1   N-Body Simulation

One naive method for achieving this simulation is to calculate the movement of a particle by accumulating the effects of pairwise particle interactions. Each pairwise interaction is calculated using Newton's laws of gravity. The acceleration a_i of a particle i due to a second particle j is determined by the equation $a_i = Gm_j/r^2$, where G is the universal gravitational constant, m_j is the mass of particle j, and r is the vector from the position of the particle i to that of particle j.

Given the acceleration of particle i at time t, the new velocity v and position p at time $t + dt$ are calculated using the equations

$$v_i^{t+dt} = v_i^t + dt a_i^t$$

$$p_i^{t+dt} = p_i^t + dt v_i^t$$

The resulting computation has complexity $O(n^2)$ since every particle is affected by the movement of every other particle.

The Barnes-Hut algorithm provides an $O(n \log n)$ alternative by using a simple idea as shown in Figure 10.1: A cluster of particles that are *far away* from a given particle can be modeled by a single particle whose mass is the total mass of the cluster and whose position is the center of mass of the cluster. The property of being far away corresponds to an *accuracy criterion* that is used for a given simulation. Program 10.1 provides an abstract outline of this algorithm.

```
For each time t
    tree=build_tree(particles)
    For each particle i^t
        if (i^t far_from tree) then
            acceleration = pairwise(i,tree)
        else
            acceleration = ∑_j acceleration(child(j,tree))
        i^{t+dt} = move(i^t,acceleration,dt)
```

Program 10.1 Abstract Formulation

At each step in the simulation a quad-tree, representing the state of the problem space, is constructed using the particles from the previous time step. Initially, the tree is empty and contains no particles. As particles are added to the tree the problem space is recursively divided, as shown in Figure 10.2(a); this is achieved by ensuring that at most one particle is present in each division of the space. As particles are added, interior nodes are used to accumulate the total mass and center of mass for each cluster of particles. Figure 10.2(b) shows the tree corresponding to the particle space shown in Figure 10.2(a). Each leaf node is a particle; each interior node represents the cumulative mass and position of all particles below it.

After the tree is constructed the acceleration of a given particle is computed by descending the tree and applying the accuracy criterion at each node. If a node provides a sufficiently accurate approximation to the effects on a particle, then the acceleration is computed by a pairwise interaction of the particle and the node. Otherwise, the contribution of a node is calculated by summing the contributions of the four children of the node.

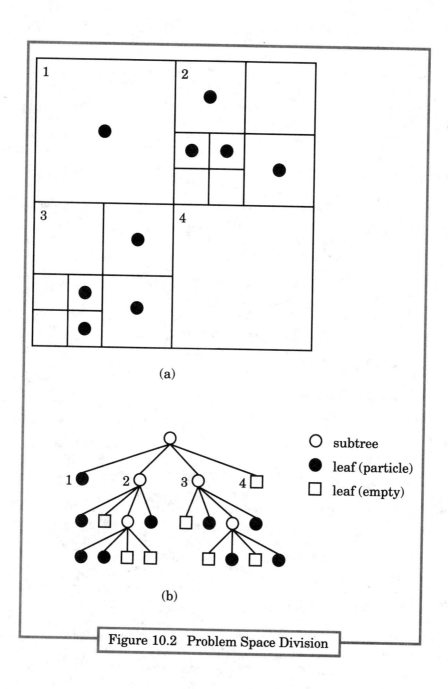

Figure 10.2   Problem Space Division

10.2   Tree-Building Refinement

In contrast to our previous designs, we here focus on the central data structures and associated operations involved in the problem. Having isolated these structures and operations, we encapsulate them within unique programs so as to hide their internal form. This technique is termed *information hiding* and yields designs that are more modular, maintainable and concurrent.

We choose to represent the particle space by a quad-tree of concurrent *node* programs that communicate by sending messages. A portion of the space containing no particles is represented by a *null* node. A portion containing a single particle is represented by a *leaf* node. A subdivision of the space is represented by a *subtree* node with associated children corresponding to the contents of the subdivisions. Consider the problem of building a quad-tree given a collection of particles. Beginning with an empty space, there are three transitions central to this activity:

1. Adding a particle to an unoccupied area of the space; this involves occupying the area with the particle as shown in Figure 10.3(a).

2. Adding a particle to an area of the space occupied by another particle. This involves dividing the area into four parts. Both particles are then *added* to the appropriate subdivision as shown in Figure 10.3(b).

3. Adding a particle to an area of the space that has already been subdivided. This involves *adding* the particle to the appropriate subdivision as shown in Figure 10.3(c).

Program 10.2 implements these transitions. Initially, the entire space contains no particles and is thus represented by a single null node. A particle is added to the space by sending it to the initial tree in a message.

The first transition involves adding a particle to an unoccupied area of the space. This corresponds to a null node receiving a particle; the corresponding action is to generate a leaf node (1). The second transition involves adding a particle to an area of the space occupied by another particle. This corresponds to a leaf node receiving a particle (2); the corresponding action is to subdivide the space (3). The subdivision is represented by a subtree (5) with four null children corresponding to empty quadrants (7). The subtree is initialized with a zero mass and position (4). Both particles involved in the transition are then *distributed* to the appropriate quadrant (5); this is achieved by a distributor program associated with each subtree (6,12). The final transition involves adding a particle to an area of subdivided space. This corresponds to a subtree receiving a particle (8); the associated action is to send the particle to the appropriate quadrant, via a distributor (9), and update the subtree mass and position (10). Notice that while null and leaf nodes only make a single transition, subtrees repeatedly receive and process particles, thus accumulating the point mass for an entire region of the space (11).

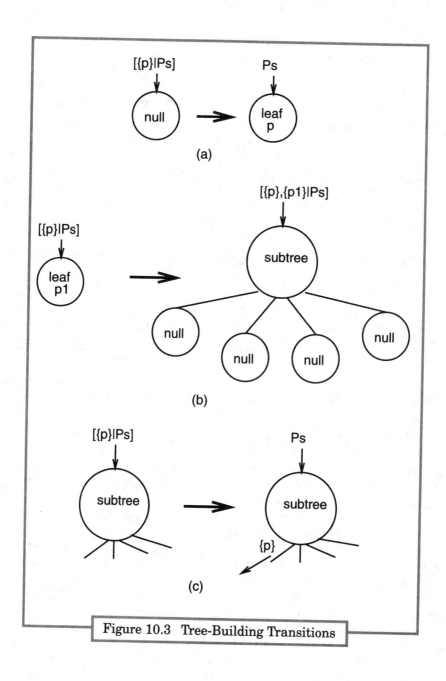

Figure 10.3 Tree-Building Transitions

```
null(Ps,space)
{ ? Ps ?= [{p} | Ps1] -> leaf(Ps1,p,space),                    /* 1 */
    .
    .
    .
}

leaf(Ps,p,space)
{ ? Ps ?= [{p1} | Ps1] ->                                      /* 2 */
        {|| cut_space(space,s0,s1,s2,s3),                       /* 3 */
            zero(zp),                                           /* 4 */
            subtree([{p},{p1} | Ps1],Ls,zp,space),             /* 5 */
            distribute(Ls,C0,C1,C2,C3),                        /* 6 */
            null(C0,s0), null(C1,s1), null(C2,s2), null(C3,s3)  /* 7 */
        },
    .
    .
    .
}

subtree(Ps,Ls,p,space)
{ ? Ps ?= [{p1} | Ps1] ->                                      /* 8 */
        {|| quadrant(p1,space,n), Ls=[{n,p1} | Ls1],           /* 9 */
            update(p,p1,p2),                                   /* 10 */
            subtree(Ps1,Ls1,p2,space)                          /* 11 */
        },
    .
    .
    .
}

distribute(Ds,O0,O1,O2,O3)                                     /* 12 */
{ ? Ds ?= [{0,p} | Ds1] -> {|| O0=[p | O0s], distribute(Ds1,O0s,O1,O2,O3)},
    Ds ?= [{1,p} | Ds1] -> {|| O1=[p | O1s], distribute(Ds1,O0,O1s,O2,O3)},
    Ds ?= [{2,p} | Ds1] -> {|| O2=[p | O2s], distribute(Ds1,O0,O1,O2s,O3)},
    Ds ?= [{3,p} | Ds1] -> {|| O3=[p | O3s], distribute(Ds1,O0,O1,O2,O3s)}
}
```

Program 10.2 Building the Quad-Tree

10.3   Refinement to Calculate Acceleration

We now refine Program 10.2 to calculate the acceleration on each particle. The central idea in the calculation of an acceleration is to propagate the particle throughout relevant parts of the associated quad-tree. As the particle propagates, a sufficiently accurate approximation to the acceleration is accumulated. Initially, the particle is directed to the root of the tree in a message; this message contains a *hole* corresponding to the total acceleration of the particle.

Each quad-tree node-type is refined to handle an acceleration message as shown in Program 10.3. The acceleration of a particle due to a null node (i.e. empty area of space) is zero (1). The acceleration on a particle due to itself is zero (2). The acceleration of a particle due to a different particle is given by a pairwise interaction (3). The acceleration due to a subtree depends on the accuracy criterion (4). If this criterion is satisfied, signifying that the subtree is far enough from the particle being considered, then the acceleration may be approximated using a pairwise interaction (5); otherwise, it is necessary to accumulate the effects of propagating the particle into each division in the subtree (6,7).

10.4   Time-Stepping the Simulation

The only task that remains is to step the simulation in time, sending the appropriate messages to cause the tree to be built, accelerations to be generated and particles moved. Program 10.4 implements the top level of the simulation. At each time step t, the space is initially represented by a solitary null node (1) corresponding to the root of the quad-tree. A stream of messages is issued to this node that causes the tree to be constructed and the appropriate accelerations to be calculated (Mb).

Recall that for each particle it is necessary to build two messages. The first is used to build the tree, the second to compute the acceleration on the particle. To ensure that the tree is built before the accelerations are calculated, we order messages within the stream such that those for building the tree enter it first. To achieve this we use the *difference list* technique introduced in Section 3.2.7.

In the particle simulation problem, the stream to be generated can be regarded as shown in Figure 10.4. It has two segments comprising all the messages for building the tree followed by all the messages for calculating accelerations. The first segment resides between the stream beginning Sb and some imaginary point Se in the middle of the stream; the second segment resides in a continuation between some point Cb and the end of the stream Ce.

```
null(Ps,space)
{ ? :
      :
    Ps ? = [{p,a} | Ps1]  -> {|| zero(a), null(Ps1,space) }          /* 1 */
}

leaf(Ps,p,space)
{ ? :
      :
    Ps ? = [{p1,a} | Ps1]  ->
        {|| { ? p1 == p  -> zero(a),                                 /* 2 */
              default  -> pairwise(p,p1,a)                           /* 3 */
            },
            leaf(Ps1,p,space)
        }
}

subtree(Ps,Ls,p,space)
{ ? :
      :
    Ps ? = [{p1,a} | Ps1]  ->
        {|| accuracy_criterion(p1,p,space,res),                      /* 4 */
            { ? res == "far"  ->
                    {|| pairwise(p,p1,a), subtree(Ps1,Ls,p,space) }, /* 5 */
              default  ->
                    {|| Ls=[{0,{p1,a1}},{1,{p1,a2}},                 /* 6 */
                           {2,{p1,a3}},{3,{p1,a4}} | Ls1],
                        summ_accelerations(a1,a2,a3,a4,a),           /* 7 */
                        subtree(Ps1,Ls1,p,space)
                    }
            }
        }
}
```

Program 10.3 Acceleration Calculation

```
simulate(t,space,Ps,Result)
{ ? t > 0 ->
        {|| null(Mb,space),                           /* 1 */
            step(Ps,Mb,Mm,Mm,[ ],Ps1),                /* 2 */
            simulate(t-1,space,Ps1,Result)            /* 3 */
        },
      default -> Result=Ps
}

step(Ps,Sb,Se,Cb,Ce,NPs)
{ ? Ps ?= [p | Ps1] ->                                /* 5 */
        {|| Sb=[{p} | Sm],                            /* 6 */
            Cb=[{p,a} | Cm],                          /* 7 */
            move(a,p,np),                             /* 8 */
            NPs=[np | NPs1],                          /* 9 */
            step(Ps1,Sm,Se,Cm,Ce,NPs1)               /* 10 */
        },
      default -> {|| Sb=Se, Cb=Ce, NPs=[ ]}
}
```

Program 10.4 Stepping the Simulation

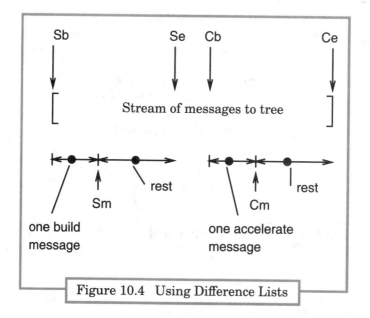

Figure 10.4 Using Difference Lists

Program 10.4 shows how the stream is assembled. To build the tree, a single message containing a particle is inserted between the beginning of the stream Sb and some intermediate point Sm (6); the remaining messages are then inserted recursively between this point and the end of the segment Se (10). Similarly, acceleration messages are inserted between the beginning of the continuation Cb and some intermediate point Cm (7); the remainder are inserted recursively between the intermediate point and the end of the stream Ce (10).

After each acceleration is generated (7), the associated particle is moved to its new position (8) and placed into the list of particles to be used on the next iteration (9).

All that remains is to ensure that the stream is eventually closed, and that the end of the stream segment for building messages corresponds to the beginning of the segment for acceleration messages. Both these requirements are achieved when a step is initialized (2).

10.5 Message Distribution

The simple distributor we have used in this chapter allows a message to be appended to one out of four streams. This design is applicable only when the number of streams is constant. It is frequently useful to be able to distribute messages to a large number of streams by indexing. This requires a more sophisticated notion of atomicity than we have used throughout this book. As a result, we here provide a sample description of how one such distributor operates; this distributor is provided as part of the PCN system.

Figure 10.5 shows a schematic for the distributor. It takes two inputs: An integer N and a stream of input messages Is. The program distributes messages occurring on the input Is to N output streams numbered 0 to N–1. There are two forms of message that may be sent to the distributor:

- attach(N1,S,D): Attach stream S to output N1 of the distributor and define D when the stream is ready for use.

- {N2,M}: Append message M to output N2 of the distributor.

These messages allow a stream to be connected to the output of the distributor and messages to be forwarded to the appropriate output via the distributor. Program 10.5 shows the final definition of tree nodes and replaces the static distributor used in Program 10.2. Initially, a distributor with four outputs is generated (1). Each output is attached to the input of a null node (2). Only when all nodes have been attached are messages forwarded via the appropriate distributor output (3).

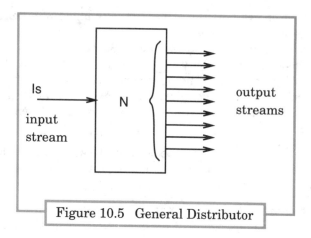

Figure 10.5   General Distributor

10.6   Summary

In this chapter we have demonstrated an alternative programming style. The central idea is to view a problem from the standpoint of its *data structures* and *associated operations*; these are collected together and *encapsulated* within individual programs. The central components of the solution, nodes in the tree, were the primary focus of the design.

This strategy yields a rather different solution, shown in Programs 10.4 and 10.5, than one would generally expect. Typically, search programs are written in terms of traversing a global state that is manipulated explicitly. In the solution presented here, the problem is solved by a collection of communicating programs. Notice that there is no explicit search algorithm; the search is encoded entirely as transitions associated with data structures.

Exercises

1. Complete the design of Programs 10.4 and 10.5.

2. Refine Programs 10.4 and 10.5 to employ a mutable state for subtree nodes.

3. Refine Programs 10.4 and 10.5 to use C-coded functions for any programs not included in the design.

4. Refine Programs 10.4 and 10.5 to operate on three-dimensional spaces.

5. Refine Programs 10.4 and 10.5 to include mapping using the bin-packing strategy.

```
null(Ps,space)
{ ? Ps ? = [{p} | Ps1] -> leaf(Ps1,p,space),
    Ps ? = [{p,a} | Ps1] -> {|| zero(a), null(Ps1,space) }
}

leaf(Ps,p,space)
{ ? Ps ? = [{p1} | Ps1] ->
        {|| cut_space(space,s0,s1,s2,s3), zero(zp),
            subtree([{p},{p1} | Ps1],Ls,zp,space),
            sys:distribute(4,ls),                               /* 1 */
            ls=[attach(0,C0,D0),attach(1,C1,D1),               /* 2 */
                attach(2,C2,D2),attach(3,C3,D3) | Rest],
            data(D0),data(D1),data(D2),data(D3) -> Rest=Ls,    /* 3 */
            null(C0,s0), null(C1,s1), null(C2,s2), null(C3,s3)
        },
    Ps ? = [{p1,a} | Ps1] ->
        {|| { ? p1 == p -> zero(a), default -> pairwise(p,p1,a) },
            leaf(Ps1,p,space)
        }
}

subtree(Ps,Ls,p,space)
{ ? Ps ? = [{p1} | Ps1] ->
        {|| quadrant(p1,space,n), Ls=[{n,p1} | Ls1],
            update(p,p1,pt2), subtree(Ps1,Ls1,pt2,space)
        },
    Ps ? = [{p1,a} | Ps1] ->
        {|| accuracy_criterion(p1,p,space,res),
            { ? res == "far" ->
                    {|| pairwise(p,p1,a), subtree(Ps1,Ls,p,space) },
                default ->
                    {|| Ls=[{0,{p1,a1}},{1,{p1,a2}},
                            {2,{p1,a3}},{3,{p1,a4}} | Ls1],
                        summ_accelerations(a1,a2,a3,a4,a),
                        subtree(Ps1,Ls1,p,space)
                    }
            }
        }
}
```

Program 10.5 Combining the Program Parts

6. Use the information hiding style to design a program that builds and maintains a balanced binary tree of numbers. The program should allow elements to be added and removed from the tree.

7. Use the information hiding style to design a concurrent program that implements Kruskal's algorithm.

8. Programs 10.4 and 10.5 suffer from the problem that if two particles are extremely close together, a deep, not particularly useful, tree is generated. Rectify this problem.

Part III

Design Theory

CHAPTER
11

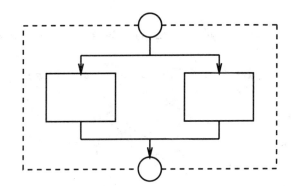

Introduction to Theory

> **Goals for this Chapter:**
>
> The goal of this chapter is to introduce you to the predicate calculus and the theory underlying the systematic design of programs.

Several books have been written on the predicate calculus, and a few pages cannot give justice to this topic. Our goal here is to give you a very elementary introduction to the subject so that you understand the chapters that follow and are motivated to study the predicate calculus further. If you have an acquaintance with formal methods you should skip this chapter.

11.1 Basic Operators

The boolean values are: true, false. We shall say that a boolean x "holds" if and only if x has value true, and we say that x "does not hold" if and only if x has value false. We introduce the monadic boolean operator (i.e. operator on a single value) $\neg$, defined as follows: $\neg x$ holds if and only if x does not hold. Read $\neg x$ as "not x" or "non x." Negation has precedence over other operators. For example, $\neg x \vee y$ means $(\neg x) \vee y$ and not $\neg(x \vee y)$.

We define the following boolean dyadic operators (i.e. operators on two values):

Conjunction. $x \wedge y$ holds if and only if x holds and y holds. Read $\wedge$ as "and."

Disjunction. $x \vee y$ holds if and only if x holds or y holds (or both hold). Read $\vee$ as "or."

Implication. $x \Rightarrow y$ holds if and only if $\neg x$ holds or y holds. Read $\Rightarrow$ as "implies." We shall say that x is "stronger than" y, and y is "weaker than" x if and only if $x \Rightarrow y$ holds.

Equivalence. Read $\equiv$ as "equivales." Equivales is also read as "if and only if." Equivalence is the same as $=$ except that the operands are boolean, and equivalence has lower binding power than the other operators, for example, by

$$x \wedge y \equiv y \wedge x$$

we mean

$$(x \wedge y) \equiv (y \wedge x)$$

and not

$$x \wedge (y \equiv y) \wedge x$$

11.2   Predicates

A predicate is a function from states of a program to booleans. (Predicates do not have to be defined in terms of program states, but in this book we do not consider any other form of predicate.) For convenience, we do not write a predicate as an explicit function on states; thus, we write V rather than $V(S)$ where S is a state and V is a predicate. Let m be an integer variable in a program. Then $m = 5$ is a predicate; it can hold in some states of the program and not hold in other states of the program. The boolean true holds in *all* states. To distinguish booleans true and false we shall refer to them as boolean scalars.

Let V be a predicate. We use the symbol $[V]$ to indicate that V holds in all states. Read $[V]$ as "everywhere V." Observe that $[V]$ is a boolean scalar and not a predicate.

Note that $[V \equiv W]$ is a stronger statement than $[V] \equiv [W]$ because the former states that the functions V and W are equivalent — for *each* state, the value of V in that state is equal to the value of W in that state — whereas the latter merely states that V holds in all states if and only if W holds in all states.

There are many beautiful theorems in the predicate calculus; next we give you a taste of some of them.

Equivalence is reflexive:

$$[\, V \equiv V \,]$$

Equivalence is symmetric (symmetric is also called commutative):

$$[(V \equiv W) \equiv (W \equiv V) \,]$$

Equivalence is associative:

$$[(U \equiv (V \equiv W)) \equiv ((U \equiv V) \equiv W)]$$

Since equivalence is associative we can dispense with the parentheses, and since it is also symmetric the order in which the operands appear is immaterial.

11.3   Quantification

Universal quantification is a generalization of conjunction and existential quantification is a generalization of disjunction. Universal and existential quantification have the form

$$(\, \forall \, dummy\_variable\_list : range : expression)$$

and

$$(\, \exists \, dummy\_variable\_list : range : expression)$$

respectively, where range, expression and the quantifications themselves are predicates, and where dummy_variable_list is an unordered list of dummy variables whose scope is the quantification, identified by the pair of parentheses.

Examples.

$$(\, \forall \, i : int(i) \wedge (0 \le i) \wedge (i < n) : x[i] = 0)$$

says that $x[i] = 0$ for all integers i in the range $0 \ldots n{-}1$.

$$(\, \exists \, i : int(i) \wedge (0 \le i) \wedge (i < n) : x[i] = 0)$$

says, there exists at least one integer i in the range $0 \ldots n{-}1$ for which $x[i] = 0$.

For convenience, the range true is omitted, and thus $(\, \forall \, i : true : f(i))$ can be written $(\, \forall \, i :: f(i))$, and $(\, \exists \, i : true : f(i))$ can be written $(\, \exists \, i :: f(i))$.

The range : expression in universal quantification is equivalent to

$$\text{true} : \text{range} \Rightarrow \text{expression}$$

For instance

$$[\, (\, \forall \, i : int(i) \wedge (0 \le i) \wedge (i < n) : x[i] = 0)$$
$$\equiv$$
$$(\, \forall \, i :: (int(i) \wedge (0 \le i) \wedge (i < n)) \Rightarrow x[i] = 0) \,]$$

Likewise, range : expression in existential quantification is equivalent to

$$\text{true} : \text{range} \wedge \text{expression}$$

For instance

$$[\, (\, \exists \, i : int(i) \wedge (0 \le i) \wedge (i < n) : x[i] = 0)$$
$$\equiv$$
$$(\, \exists \, i :: int(i) \wedge (0 \le i) \wedge (i < n) \wedge x[i] = 0) \,]$$

Let C be the index set $\{ \, j \mid int(j) \wedge (0 \le j < n) \}$, i.e. C is the set $\{0,1,\ldots,n-1\}$. Then

$$[\, (\, \forall \, i : i \in C : f(i,x)) \equiv f(0,x) \wedge f(1,x) \wedge \ldots f(n-1,x) \,]$$

and

$$[\, (\, \exists \, i : i \in C : f(i,x) \,) \equiv f(0,x) \vee f(1,x) \vee \ldots f(n-1,x) \,]$$

Thus, universal and existential quantifications are generalizations of conjunction and disjunction, respectively.

The range in a quantification may be infinite, as in:

$$[\, (\, \forall \, i : int(i) \wedge (i > 1) : i*i > i) \,]$$

Some of the theorems we use later are:

$$[\, (\, \forall \, i : f : g) \wedge (\, \forall \, i : f : h) \equiv (\, \forall \, i : f : g \wedge h) \,]$$

$$[\, (\, \forall \, i : f(i) : (\, \forall \, j : g(j) : h(i,j))) \equiv (\, \forall \, j : g(j) : (\, \forall \, i : f(i) : h(i,j) \,)) \,]$$

and

$$[\, (\, \forall \, i,j : g(i) \wedge g(j) : i = j) \,] \Rightarrow [\, (\, \exists \, i :: g(i)) \equiv (\, \exists \, i : g(i) : b(i)) \equiv (\, \forall \, i : g(i) : b(i)) \,]$$

11.4 Relations

We shall define a state transition system in the next chapter. If the system is in a state, say S, we define the possible next states that the system can enter by means of a binary relation $\rightarrow$. The relation is a set of pairs of states, and S $\rightarrow$ S' is a boolean scalar that holds if and only if the pair (S,S') is in the set. The system can transit from S to S' if and only if S $\rightarrow$ S' holds. (Relations can be of any order, but in this book we only consider binary relations.)

11.5 Introduction to Design Theory

In Chapter 12 we propose an operational semantic by defining a state transition system for PCN. Chapter 13 derives proof rules that help in proving that PCN programs satisfy their specifications. In that chapter we propose an operator called "establishes" between program blocks and predicates, where program block b establishes predicate B means (informally) that in all computations of b there will eventually come a point at which B holds and then continues to hold. The central results are as follows. Consider a program that does not use mutable variables or sequential composition. Then,

1. If program block b establishes predicate B and program block c establishes predicate C then the parallel block {|| b,c} establishes B $\wedge$ C, provided the rules for parallel composition are satisfied, i.e., no definition variable is defined in both b and c. Thus **parallel composition of programs corresponds to conjunction of specifications**.

2. With b,B,c,C defined as before, the choice composition block
$$\{ ? g \rightarrow b, h \rightarrow c\}$$
establishes $(g \vee h) \equiv (g \wedge b) \vee (h \wedge c)$. Equivalently, the choice composition block establishes $(g \vee h) \Rightarrow (g \wedge b) \vee (h \wedge c)$.

   If at most one guard holds, i.e., $\neg(g \wedge h)$, then the choice composition block establishes $(g \Rightarrow b) \wedge (h \Rightarrow c)$. Thus **choice composition corresponds to conjunction of implications if at most one guard holds**.

3. Rules are given for proving that a program terminates.

4. Rules are given for transforming a program that does not use mutable variables or sequential composition into one that does, so that the transformed program also meets the specification of the original program. These rules can be used to make programs more efficient in memory and (in some cases) in speed.

Several sample programs are designed, starting from their specifications, in a systematic manner.

Chapter 14 shows how to design and reason about reactive systems that interact with their environments. This brief introduction should be sufficient to read the remaining chapters.

CHAPTER
12

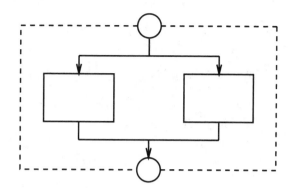

Operational Semantic

Goals for this Chapter:

This chapter gives the operational semantic of PCN programs. By the end of this chapter you should understand how the operation of a parallel program is described formally in terms of a state-transition system.

The meaning of a program in terms of its operation is called its **operational semantic**. The meaning of a program in terms of syntactic proof rules that relate program statements to predicates, and that allow us to prove that a program satisfies its specification, is called its **axiomatic semantic**. An axiomatic semantic is described in the next chapter.

We describe the operation of a program in terms of a model called an **operational model**. The operational model we use is called the **state-transition system** model, or **transition system**.

12.1   Transition Systems

A **transition system** is defined by
1. a nonempty set of **states**,
2. a subset of the set of states called the set of **initial** states,
3. a binary relation $\rightarrow$ (called **transition**) between states, and
4. a **fairness** rule.

We use letters S and T for states. We define a **final state** as follows:

$$\text{S is a final state} \equiv \neg\,(\,\exists\,T :: S \rightarrow T)$$

12.1.1   Maximal Computation

A **maximal computation** of a program is
1. a finite nonempty sequence $(S_i, 0 \leq i \leq k)$ of states, where S_0 is an initial state, and S_k is a final state, and $(\forall i : 0 \leq i < k : S_i \rightarrow S_{i+1})$, or
2. a fair infinite sequence $(S_i, 0 \leq i)$ of states, where S_0 is an initial state, and $(\forall i : 0 \leq i : S_i \rightarrow S_{i+1})$. Fairness is defined later.

A computation is any initial subsequence (including the empty subsequence) of a maximal computation.

12.1.2   Informal Explanation

A state of a system is its memory; the future behavior of a system, given its current state, is independent of its past behavior. A transition system is defined by the states of a system, the set of initial states, the allowable transitions between states, and a fairness rule. If a system is started in an initial state, it will either make a finite sequence of state transitions and end in a final state – a state without outgoing transitions – or it will make an infinite sequence of state transitions. The fairness rule restricts the infinite sequences of transitions that can be made. A maximal computation is the sequence of states of a system, started in an initial state, where the sequence is either infinite or terminates in a final state.

12.2   States

12.2.1   Variables

A variable in a PCN program is either a mutable variable or a definition variable. A mutable variable is the same as a variable in imperative languages such as Pascal, C or Fortran. A definition variable is initially undefined, and can be defined (i.e. assigned a value) at most once. A definition variable does not have a value until it is defined; its value is called its **definition**. A definition is an expression or tuple that does not name mutables (but can name definition variables). A tuple is a sequence of items between braces "{" and "}" where an item is a number, boolean scalar (true or false), string, variable, expression, or tuple. Items in a sequence are separated by commas. (Boolean scalars in PCN are treated as in C, i.e. zero (0) is equal to false and nonzero to true.)

A list is a special case of a tuple; a list is either the empty tuple {} or it is a two-tuple {a,b} where b is a list; a is the head of the list and b is the tail (the remainder) of the list. For convenience, PCN has an alternate notation for lists: A list is a sequence of tuple-items enclosed between brackets "[" and "]", or it is of the form [u | v] where u is a sequence of one or more tuple-items and v is a tuple-item. If u is a singleton sequence a, i.e., a sequence consisting of a single item a, then [u | v] is equivalent to {a,v}. If u is a sequence with more than one item, let a be the first item of u and let b be the remainder of u; then [u | v] is equivalent to {a,[b | v]}.

We use the notation "v $\stackrel{\text{def}}{=}$ e in S" for "v **is defined as** e **in state** S," and we use "$\mathcal{U}$.v in S" for "v **is undefined in state** S." The relation $\stackrel{\text{def}}{=}$ is not symmetric; for instance it is possible that $(x \stackrel{\text{def}}{=} y) \wedge \neg (y \stackrel{\text{def}}{=} x)$ in a state.

12.2.2   The State of a Program

The state of a PCN program is given by

1. a set M of mutable variables, and a set D of definition variables,

2. a value for each mutable variable in M,

3. for each definition variable v in D:

   (a) a boolean $\mathcal{U}$.v, and

   (b) a (single) definition for v if and only if $\neg \mathcal{U}$.v holds, and

4. a set C of **points of execution** in the program; this set is called the **candidate set**.

A point of execution is a point in the text of a program p and the context of the execution of p. The context of an execution of p defines the binding between actual parameters in the call to p with the formal parameters of p, and defines the sequence of program calls that led to the execution of p. Sequential programs have a single *location counter* in place of the candidate set.

12.2.3   Definitions, Reductions and Ground Values

We use the notation [X] for "predicate X holds in all states of the program." From the meaning of undefined, we have

$$[\,(\exists\, e:: x \stackrel{\text{def}}{=} e) \equiv \neg_{\iota}(\mathcal{U}.x)\,]$$

If x is defined as e in a state, then x equals e in that state:

$$[\,(x \stackrel{\text{def}}{=} e) \Rightarrow (x = e)\,]$$

It is possible, however, that in some state, $(x = y) \wedge \neg (x \stackrel{\text{def}}{=} y)$ because, for instance, $(y \stackrel{\text{def}}{=} x) \wedge \neg (x \stackrel{\text{def}}{=} y)$.

Reduction. We introduce a binary relation ∼, called **reduces to** between definition variables and expressions or tuples. It is defined as the strongest solution of

$$[\,(x \sim e) \equiv ((x \stackrel{\text{def}}{=} e) \vee (\exists\, f, y, g :: (x \sim f) \wedge (y \stackrel{\text{def}}{=} g) \wedge (e = f_g^y)))\,]$$

where f_g^y is obtained by substituting g for all occurrences of y in f.

In other words, x ∼ e if and only if x is defined as e, or x is defined as f and repeatedly substituting definitions for variables in f gives e.

Ground Values. A **ground value** is a number, a boolean constant (i.e., true or false) or a string. For a definition variable x we introduce the predicate data.x, where data.x holds if and only if x reduces to a ground value or a tuple.

$$[\,\text{data.x} \equiv (\exists\, w: w \text{ is a ground value or tuple} : x \sim w)\,]$$

Likewise, we introduce the predicate $\mathcal{G}.x$ where $\mathcal{G}.x$ holds if and only if x reduces to a ground value.

$$[\,\mathcal{G}.x \equiv (\exists\, w: w \text{ is a ground value} : x \sim w)\,]$$

From the definitions, $\mathcal{G}.x$ is stronger than data.x:

$$[\,\mathcal{G}.x \Rightarrow \text{data.x}\,]$$

12.3 Statements

For convenience, some of the PCN syntax is given here.

PCN-program ::
     program-name(formal-parameter-list)
     declaration-section
     block

block ::
     definition-statement |
     assignment-statement |
     program-call |
     composed-block

composed-block :: parallel-block | choice-block | sequential-block

A definition statement has the syntax $x = e$, where x is a definition variable and e is an expression or tuple or list — recall that a list is a special case of a tuple. An assignment statement has the syntax $m := e$, where m is a mutable variable and e is an expression.

The syntax for parallel, choice and sequential blocks is {|| block-list }, { ? guarded-block-list} and { ; block-list }, respectively, where block-list is a list of one or more blocks, and likewise, a guarded-block-list is a list of one or more guarded-blocks, where a guarded-block is guard –> block. Here we extend the syntax of composed blocks to:

$$\{ || \, i : i \in K : a_i \}, \text{ and } \{ \, ? \, i : i \in K : g_i -> a_i \}, \text{ and } \{ \, ; \, i : 0 \leq i < n : a_i \}$$

for parallel, choice and sequential blocks, respectively, where K is a constant finite nonempty set of indexes, and n is a constant positive integer. Here a_i is a block, and g_i is a guard. The parallel block is a parallel composition of blocks a_i for all i in K. Likewise, the choice block is the choice composition of guarded blocks $g_i -> a_i$ for all i in K and the sequential block is the sequential composition of the ordered list of blocks $a_0,\ldots, a_{n-1}$.

Parallel and choice composition are associative and symmetric whereas sequential composition is not symmetric. The notation {|| a,b,c,d } is a syntactically convenient form of (a || b || c || d), treating || as a binary operator on program blocks. Hence, for instance, {|| a, {|| b,c } } is the same as {|| c, {|| b,a } }.

An execution point is at the initiation or termination of a block. For brevity, we represent an execution point at the initiation and termination of a block b by $I.b$ and $T.b$, respectively, and we do not give the context of the execution of b explicitly.

12.4   Transitions

Next we define S → S'. Let M, D, C be the set of mutable variables, the set of definition variables, and the candidate set in state S, respectively, and let M', D', C' be the corresponding sets in S'. Let V = M $\cup$ D, and let V' be the corresponding set in S'.

We introduce a boolean function same on a variable v and states S and S', defined as follows:

$$\begin{aligned} &\text{same(v,S,S')}\\ \equiv\ &((v \in M \cap M') \wedge ((v{=}y \text{ in S}) \equiv (v{=}y \text{ in S'})))\\ &\vee\\ &((v \in D \cap D') \wedge ((v \stackrel{\text{def}}{=} f \text{ in S}) \equiv (v \stackrel{\text{def}}{=} f \text{ in S'}))) \end{aligned}$$

Thus same(v,S,S') holds if and only if variable v has the same value or definition in both states S and S'.

We introduce another boolean function identical_variables on states S and S' defined as follows:

$$\text{identical\_variables(S,S')} \equiv (M = M') \wedge (D = D') \wedge (\forall v : v \in V : \text{same(v,S,S')})$$

Hence, identical_variables(S,S') holds if and only if all variables have the same values or definitions in both states, S and S'.

We define → as follows:

$$\begin{aligned} \text{S} \rightarrow \text{S'}\ \equiv\ &\text{execute\_definition\_statement(S,S')}\\ &\vee \text{execute\_assignment\_statement(S,S')}\\ &\vee \text{initiate\_PCN\_program(S,S')}\\ &\vee \text{terminate\_PCN\_program(S,S')}\\ &\vee \text{execute\_foreign\_program(S,S')}\\ &\vee \text{initiate\_parallel\_block(S,S')}\\ &\vee \text{within\_parallel\_block(S,S')}\\ &\vee \text{terminate\_parallel\_block(S,S')}\\ &\vee \text{initiate\_sequential\_block(S,S')}\\ &\vee \text{within\_sequential\_block(S,S')}\\ &\vee \text{terminate\_sequential\_block(S,S')}\\ &\vee \text{initiate\_choice\_block(S,S')}\\ &\vee \text{terminate\_choice\_block(S,S')} \end{aligned}$$

The functions execute_definition_statement, through terminate_choice_block are defined next.

Execute Definition Statement.

We define execute_definition_statement(S,S') as follows: There exists a definition statement x = e where

$$(M = M') \wedge (D = D') \wedge (\forall v : v \in V\text{--}x : same(v,S,S')) \wedge$$
$$(I.(x = e) \in C) \wedge (C' = C + T.(x = e) - I.(x = e)) \wedge (x \stackrel{\text{def}}{=} e' \text{ in } S')$$

where

1. if ($\mathcal{U}.x$ in S) then e' is obtained by substituting for each mutable variable
   w in e, the value of w in S, and

2. if $\neg$ ($\mathcal{U}.x$ in S) then e' is arbitrary.

Informal Explanation: If a point of execution is at the initiation of a definition
statement x = e in a state S in which x is undefined, then there can be a
transition from S in which the point of execution moves from the initiation of
the statement x = e to the termination of the statement, and x becomes defined
as e'. If x is defined in S then x becomes redefined as an arbitrary value. (We
will design programs in which each definition variable is defined at most once
in an execution.)

Execute Assignment Statement.

We define execute_assignment_statement(S,S') as follows: There exists an assignment statement m := e where:

$$(M = M') \wedge (D = D') \wedge (\forall v : v \in V\text{--}m: same(v,S,S')) \wedge$$
$$(I.(m := e) \in C) \wedge (C' = C + T.(m := e) - I.(m := e)) \wedge$$
$$(\forall x : (x \in D) \wedge (x \text{ appears in } e) : data.x \text{ in } S) \wedge (m = e' \text{ in } S')$$

where e' is obtained from e by substituting for each mutable variable in e
its value in S, and substituting for each definition variable x in e the ground
value to which x reduces in S. (If a definition variable x appearing in e reduces
to a tuple in S, then e' is arbitrary because tuples or expressions that name
tuples should not be assigned to mutables. Likewise, any error in evaluating
e' results in e' being an arbitrary value.)

Informal Explanation: A point of execution can move from the initiation of
an assignment statement m := e to the termination of the statement, if all
definition variables in e reduce to ground values (or to tuples); after this transition the value of m changes to e'. If some definition variable in e does not

reduce to a ground value or tuple in state S then there is no transition from S corresponding to the execution of the assignment statement m := e.

Initiate PCN Program Call.

We define initiate_PCN_program(S,S') as follows: There exists a call p(x) to a PCN program p where x is the sequence of actual parameters of the call, where

$$(M' = M \cup u) \wedge (D' = D \cup t) \wedge (\forall y : y \in t : (\mathcal{U}.y \text{ in } S')) \wedge$$
$$(\forall v : v \in V: \text{same}(v,S,S')) \wedge (I.p(x) \in C) \wedge (C' = C + I.b - I.p(x))$$

where u is the set of local mutable variables of p, and t is the set of local definition variables of p and the body of program p is block b.

Informal Explanation: A point of execution moves from the initiation of a program call to the initiation of the body (the block) of the called program, and the context of the block is set up. Local variables of the called program are accessible in state S'. All local definition variables of the called program are undefined, and local mutable variables have arbitrary value, in S'.

Of course, each call to the same program results in fresh (different) local variables becoming instantiated. We do not give a naming convention to distinguish fresh instances of local variables. (One naming convention is to prefix each variable name with the sequence of program calls that led to its instantiation.)

Actual parameters of the call are bound to formal parameters. Values and definitions of all variables, other than local variables of p, are the same in states S and S'.

Terminate PCN Program Call.

We define terminate_PCN_program(S,S') as follows: There exists p, x, u, t, b as in the previous paragraph, with

$$(M' = M - u) \wedge (D' = D - t) \wedge (\forall v : v \in V': \text{same}(v,S,S')) \wedge$$
$$(T.b \in C) \wedge (C' = C + T.p(x) - T.b)$$

Informal Explanation: A point of execution moves from terminating a block b which is the body of a program p to terminating the call to p. Local variables of p are not accessible after the transition.

Execute a non-PCN Program.

We define execute_foreign_program(S,S') as follows: There exists a call p(x) to a program p in C, Fortran, or some notation other than PCN, where x is the sequence of actual parameters of the call and where

$$(M = M') \wedge (D = D') \wedge (\forall v : v \text{ does not appear in } x: \text{same}(v,S,S')) \wedge$$
$$(I.p(x) \in C) \wedge (C' = C + T.p(x) - I.p(x)) \wedge$$
$$(\forall w : (w \in D) \wedge (w \text{ appears in } x): (\text{data.w in S}) \wedge (w \stackrel{\text{def}}{=} w' \text{ in } S')) \wedge$$
$$(\forall v : (v \in M) \wedge (v \text{ appears in } x): v = v' \text{ in } S')$$

where v' is defined as follows: For a mutable variable v, v' is the value assigned to v by the call p(x) when the call terminates; we do not give the semantics of program calls in notations other than PCN — we assume that the value of a variable in a program in Fortran, C, or some other notation, upon termination of the program, is defined in some manner.

If a definition variable w is modified by p(x) then w' is arbitrary, and if it is left unmodified by p(x) then w' is the definition of w in state S. Of course, we take care to design programs in which definition variables are left unmodified by non-PCN programs.

Informal Explanation: If a definition variable in the sequence of actual parameters x does not reduce to a ground value or tuple in state S then there is no transition from S corresponding to executing the program call p(x). If all definition variables in x reduce to ground values or tuples, then there is a transition from S corresponding to executing p(x) with actual definition parameters replaced by the ground values or tuples to which they reduce. In this transition, a point of control moves from initiating p(x) to terminating p(x).

The execution of p(x) is treated as an atomic operation. We restrict attention to programs p that terminate and have no side effects. After completion of p(x) the values of mutables in x are as specified by p(x) and the values of definition variables in x are unchanged if not modified by p(x), and are arbitrary if modified by p(x).

Initiate Parallel Block.

We define initiate_parallel_block(S,S') as follows: There exists a block b where b is $\{|| i : i \in K : a_i \}$ and where

$$\text{identical\_variables}(S,S') \wedge (I.b \in C) \wedge (C' = C \cup \{I.a_i \mid i \in K\} - I.b)$$

Informal Explanation: A point of execution moves from the initiation of a parallel block, and spawns one point of execution at the initiation of each of the constituent blocks. Variables remain unchanged.

Within Parallel Block.

We define within_parallel_block(S,S') as follows: There exists a block b where b is $\{\,\|\,i : i \in K : a_i\,\}$ and where

$$
\begin{aligned}
&\text{identical\_variables(S,S')} \wedge \\
&(\exists i : i \in K : (T.a_i \in C) \wedge \\
&(\exists j : (j \in K) \wedge (j \neq i) : \text{executing.}a_j \text{ in S}) \wedge (C' = C - T.a_i))
\end{aligned}
$$

where executing.a_j in S holds if and only if ($a_j \in C$) or a_j is a composed block, and there is a constituent block d of a_j where executing.d in S, or a_j is a program call and the body of a_j is a block d and executing.d in S.

Informal Explanation: This transition corresponds to the termination of one of the constituent blocks a_i of a parallel block b in a state in which there is at least one other constituent block a_j executing; in this case the parallel block remains in execution. Variables remain unchanged.

Terminate Parallel Block.

We define terminate_parallel_block(S,S') as follows: There exists a block b where b is $\{\,\|\,i : i \in K : a_i\}$ and where

$$
\begin{aligned}
&\text{identical\_variables(S,S')} \wedge \\
&(\exists i : i \in K : (T.a_i \in C) \wedge \\
&(\forall j : (j \in K) \wedge (j \neq i) : \neg(\text{executing.}a_j \text{ in S})) \wedge (C' = C + T.b - T.a_i))
\end{aligned}
$$

Informal Explanation: This transition corresponds to the case where a constituent block a_i of a parallel block b terminates execution after all other constituent blocks a_j of b have terminated execution; in this case a point of control moves from the termination of a_i to the termination of the parallel block b. Variables remain unchanged.

Initiate Sequential Block.

We define initiate_sequential_block(S,S') as follows: There exists a block b where b is $\{\,;\,i : 0 \leq i < n : a_i\}$ and where

$$identical\_variables(S,S') \wedge (I.b \in C) \wedge (C' = C + I.a_0 - I.b)$$

Informal Explanation: A point of execution moves from the initiation of a sequential block b to the initiation of the first constituent block a_0 within it, leaving variables unchanged.

Within Sequential Block.

We define within_sequential_block(S,S') as follows: There exists a block b where b is { ; i : 0 ≤ i < n : a_i} and where

$$identical\_variables(S,S') \wedge$$
$$(\exists i: 0 \le i < n-1 : (T.a_i \in C) \wedge (C' = C + I.a_{i+1} - T.a_i))$$

Informal Explanation: A point of execution moves from terminating one constituent block a_i of a sequential block to initiating the next constituent block a_{i+1}, where i < n−1, leaving variables unchanged.

Terminate Sequential Block.

We define terminate_sequential_block(S,S') as follows: There exists a block b where b is { ; i : 0 ≤ i < n : a_i} and where

$$identical\_variables(S,S') \wedge (T.a_{n-1} \in C) \wedge (C' = C + T.b - T.a_{n-1})$$

Informal Explanation: A point of control moves from terminating the last constituent block of a sequential block to terminating the sequential block itself leaving variables unchanged.

Initiate Choice Block.

We define initiate_choice_block(S,S') as follows: There exists a block b where b is { ? i : i ∈ K : g_i –> a_i} and where

$$identical\_variables(S,S') \wedge (I.b \in C) \wedge$$
$$(((\forall i : i \in K : g_i \sim false) \wedge (C' = C + T.b - I.b)) \vee$$
$$(\exists i : i \in K : (g_i \sim true) \wedge (C' = C + I.a_i - I.b)))$$

Informal Explanation: A point of execution moves from initiating a choice block to terminating the block if all guards reduce to false. If a guard reduces to true, then the point of execution moves from initiating the choice block to initiating any block guarded by a guard that reduces to true. If no guard reduces to true, and at least one guard does not reduce to false, then there is no transition from state S corresponding to the initiation of the choice block.

Terminate Choice Block.

We define terminate_choice_block(S,S') as follows: There exists a block b where b is $\{ \, ? \, i : i \in K : g_i \rightarrow a_i \}$ and where

$$\text{identical\_variables(S,S')} \land (\exists j : j \in K : (\mathcal{T}.a_j \in C) \land (C' = C + \mathcal{T}.b - \mathcal{T}.a_j))$$

Informal Explanation: A point of execution moves from terminating one of the blocks a_j within a choice block to terminating the choice block itself, leaving variables unchanged.

Guards. A guard is a sequence of one or more guard elements, where guard elements are separated by commas. If a guard, or a guard element, reduces to a ground value then it reduces either to true or to false. Let H be a sequence of guard elements, and let $\mathcal{F}.H$ be the value that H reduces to. Let g be a guard element. We define $\mathcal{F}$ as follows:

$$[(g \sim \text{true}) \Rightarrow (\mathcal{F}.(g,H) \equiv \mathcal{F}.H)]$$
$$[(g \sim \text{false}) \Rightarrow (\mathcal{F}.(g,H) \equiv \text{false})]$$
$$[\neg\, \mathcal{G}.g \Rightarrow \neg\, \mathcal{G}.(g,H)]$$

and an empty sequence of guard elements reduces to true.

Informal Explanation: Guard elements in a guard are evaluated from left to right while guard elements reduce to true, until (1) all guard elements reduce to true, in this case the guard reduces to true, or (2) a guard element reduces to false, in this case the guard reduces to false, or (3) a guard-element does not reduce to a ground value, in this case the guard does not reduce to a ground value.

Guard Elements. A guard element is a comparison between two variables or values, or it is an equality test or a pattern match. A comparison has the form x op y where op is $<\,,\,>\,,\,<=\,,\,>=\,$, or $!=$ (where $!=$ stands for "not equal to"). The rule for reduction of comparisons is as follows

$$[\, (\text{data.x} \land \text{data.y} \equiv \mathcal{G}.(x \text{ op } y)) \,]$$

Informal Explanation: If x and y reduce to ground values x' and y' respectively, then x op y reduces to the value of x' op y'. If x or y reduces to a tuple, then x op y reduces to an unspecified value; we do not specify the value because we design programs in which tuples are not compared.

Pattern Matches. A pattern match is of the form x ? = pat, where pat is a **pattern**. A pattern is sequence of dummy variables or patterns between braces { and } or between brackets [and]. A pattern match x ? = pat reduces to true if and only if x reduces to a tuple of the same **shape** as pat; the pattern match reduces to false if and only if x reduces to a ground value or to a tuple of different shape than the pattern. A tuple t has the same shape as a pattern p if and only if the number of elements of t (its size) is the same as that of p, and for each element of p either the element is a dummy variable, or it is a pattern q and the corresponding element of t is a tuple that has the same shape as q.

Equality Test. An equality test is of the form x == y, where x and y are variables or ground values. An equality test x == y reduces to true if and only if both x and y reduce to identical ground values or grounded tuples. A grounded tuple is a tuple, all of whose elements are ground values or grounded tuples. The equality test x == y reduces to false if and only if x and y reduce to different ground values or grounded tuples, or if the operands reduce to tuples of different shapes, or if one operand reduces to a tuple and the other to a ground value.

12.5 Fairness

We define **executable** points of execution as follows:

$$(p \text{ is executable in } S) \equiv (p \in C) \land (\exists S' : S \to S' : \neg (p \in C'))$$

A point of execution p is executable in a state S if and only if p is in the candidate set of S, and there is a transition from S to a state S' where p is not in the candidate set of S'.

A sequence, $(S_i, i \geq 0)$, of states is **fair** if and only if for all i, $i \geq 0$, and for all points of execution p executable in state S_i, there exists j, $j > i$, such that p is not executable in S_j.

12.6 Summary

In this chapter we gave an operational semantic for PCN by defining its transition system. An operational semantic can be used to reason about programs, though we often find an axiomatic semantic more convenient for this purpose.

Exercises

1. The meaning of programs min4 and sum in Chapter 2 were given, informally, in terms of operational semantics. Define the transition system
   for these two programs for the arguments given in Tables 2.1 and 2.2
   respectively. You do not have to define the entire transition system for
   these programs, because it is quite long; it is sufficient if you describe a
   part of the system.

2. Define the transition system for the bubble sort in Chapter 4 for the input
   sequence defined in Figure 4.2.

3. Attempt to define the program for the grid problem in Chapter 8. You will
   find the transition system to be large and cumbersome. Therefore, you
   will find formal reasoning about the transition system to be cumbersome
   as well. Try to give an argument to show that the program is correct.

CHAPTER

13

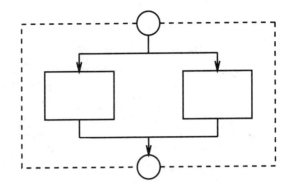

Design Methods

Goals for this Chapter:

The goal of this chapter is to introduce you to systematic methods for developing parallel programs. You will learn that most of your effort in developing parallel programs is in structuring complex specifications as compositions of simpler specifications. You will be introduced to proof rules that help you to design correct parallel programs.

We develop programs in the following way:

1. Given a sufficiently simple specification, we derive a program from it in a simple mechanical fashion.

2. Given a complex specification, we show that it is composed of simpler specifications. The operators for composing specifications are logical and, logical or and implies. We can obtain a program that satisfies a composition of simpler specifications by composing programs that satisfy the simpler specifications. We demonstrate a relationship between the way in which specifications are composed and the way in which programs are composed.

> **Specification Composition:** Most of your effort in developing parallel programs is in showing that complex specifications are compositions of simpler specifications.

We show that composition of specifications using conjunction corresponds to composition of programs using parallel composition. Also composition of specifications using implications corresponds to composition of programs using choice composition. Thus program structure corresponds to specification structure.

One advantage of structuring specifications into compositions of simple specifications is that most of your work will not depend very much on the target programming language or architecture. If you have to rewrite your program in a different language, you will find your task easier if you have already structured your specification as a composition of simpler specifications.

You do not have to be concerned with the operational steps of a program (its operational semantic) in program development. This chapter shows you how to refine specifications and then transform them into programs in a mechanical fashion, by using syntactic rules, called **proof rules**.

Though the design strategy proposed here borrows a great deal from functional programming, some of the programs developed in this book are not functional: they can be nondeterministic. A function is a mapping from inputs to outputs: for a given input there is at most one output. By contrast, in nondeterministic programs, there can be more than one output for a given input. Therefore, our design strategy is based on the predicate calculus, because it allows us to work with relations between inputs and outputs, and not only with functions from inputs to outputs.

> **Design Methods:** Our design methods are based on the predicate calculus, because doing so allows us to work with relations between inputs and outputs, and not just with functions from inputs to outputs.

Transformational and Reactive Programs. Sequential programs are usually **transformational** programs, i.e., their specifications are given in terms of states at the beginning and at the end of program execution. We care about interactions between a **reactive** program and its environment *while the program is executing.* A reactive program, such as an operating system, may never terminate, so we cannot specify a reactive program by its states at the beginning and at the end of program execution.

In this book we develop both reactive programs and transformational programs though our emphasis is on transformational programs. This chapter is concerned with transformational programs; Chapter 14 deals with reactive programs.

13.1   Predicates Established by Blocks

Definition of Proper. A maximal computation of a parallel block $\{|| \, i : i \in K : b_i \}$ is **proper** if and only if

1. the same definition variable is not defined in distinct blocks b_i and b_j in the computation, and

2. no mutable variable that appears in distinct blocks b_i and b_j is modified in the computation.

We design parallel blocks so that all their maximal computations are proper.

Definition of Establishes. A block b **establishes** a predicate B if and only if for all blocks p and all proper maximal computations of $\{|| \, p,b\}$, after a finite number of transitions, B holds and continues to hold forever thereafter.

Form of Specifications. In this chapter, our specifications have the following form: Given a predicate, derive a program that establishes it.

Next, we restrict attention to programs using only definition variables, parallel composition and choice composition and derive proof rules from the operational semantic. You can skip the theorems on a first reading and go directly to the summary of proof rules in the next section.

13.2   Theorems

We introduce a binary relation final between a predicate X and a nonempty sequence T of states as follows:

$$X \text{ final } T \equiv (\exists j : (0 \leq j < \text{length}.T) \land (j \text{ is finite}) : (\forall i : j \leq i : X \text{ holds in } T_i))$$

where length.T is the number of elements in sequence T (which can be infinite), and T_i is the i-th element of T, for $0 \leq i < \text{length}.T$. Note that states in T are indexed starting from zero and not from one.

Thus X final T holds if and only if

1. T is a finite sequence and X holds in the final state of T, or
2. T is an infinite sequence and after a finite number of state transitions X holds and continues to hold forever thereafter.

From the definition of final

$$(\text{false final } T) \equiv \text{false}$$
$$(\text{true final } T) \equiv \text{true}$$

We adapt the Dijkstra-Scholten proof notation, using ordinary font for hints.

Theorem 1: $((X \text{ final } T) \wedge (Y \text{ final } T)) \equiv ((X \wedge Y) \text{ final } T)$

Proof: We first prove: $((X \text{ final } T) \wedge (Y \text{ final } T)) \Rightarrow ((X \wedge Y) \text{ final } T)$

From the definition of final

$$X \text{ final } T \equiv (\exists j : (0 \le j < \text{length}.T) \wedge \text{finite } j : (\forall i : j \le i : X \text{ holds in } T_i))$$
$$Y \text{ final } T \equiv (\exists k : (0 \le k < \text{length}.T) \wedge \text{finite } k : (\forall i : k \le i : Y \text{ holds in } T_i))$$

Let J, K be values of j, k respectively, that satisfy the expressions in the quantification, and let $m = \max(J,K)$. Then

$$(0 \le m < \text{length}.T) \wedge \text{finite } m.$$

$\quad ((X \text{ final } T) \wedge (Y \text{ final } T))$
$\Rightarrow \quad$ from the last three equations,
$\quad ((\forall i : m \le i : X \text{ holds in } T_i) \wedge (\forall i : m \le i : Y \text{ holds in } T_i))$
$\equiv \quad$ because universal quantifications with same range distribute over $\wedge$,
$\quad ((\forall i : m \le i : (X \wedge Y) \text{ holds in } T_i)$
$\Rightarrow \quad$ from definition of final
$\quad ((X \wedge Y) \text{ final } T)$

Proof: $((X \wedge Y) \text{ final } T) \Rightarrow ((X \text{ final } T) \wedge (Y \text{ final } T))$ follows directly from the definition of final.

This theorem deals with the conjunction of *two* predicates; the next theorem extends the result to a conjunction of an arbitrary finite number of predicates.

Theorem 2: For any finite set V of predicates

$$((\forall X : X \in V : X) \text{ final } T) \equiv (\forall X : X \in V : X \text{ final } T)$$

Proof: By induction on the cardinality of V, using the previous theorem.

We use $\star$ for **establishes**; hence

$\equiv$

   $b \star X$

   $(\forall p : p$ is a block :
   $(\forall T : T$ is a proper maximal computation of $\{ ||\, p,b \} : X$ final $T))$

Thus $b \star X$ holds if and only if, in all proper maximal computations of a parallel composition of b with other blocks,

1. the maximal computation is finite and X holds in the final state, or

2. the maximal computation is infinite and X holds, and continues to hold, after a finite number of state transitions.

From the definition of $\star$, $(b \star$ false$) \equiv$ false.

The next three theorems prove that parallel composition of a set of blocks establishes the conjunction of the predicates established by each of the constituent blocks.

Theorem 3: For any finite set V of predicates,

$$(b \star (\forall X : X \in V : X)) \equiv (\forall X : X \in V : b \star X)$$

Proof:

   $b \star (\forall X : X \in V : X)$
$\equiv$ because of definition of $\star$
   $(\forall p : p$ is a block : $(\forall T : T$ is a proper maximal computation of $\{ ||\, p,b \} :$
   $(\forall X : X \in V : X)$ final $T))$
$\equiv$ from theorem 2
   $(\forall p : p$ is a block : $(\forall T : T$ is a proper maximal computation of $\{ ||\, p,b \} :$
   $(\forall X : X \in V : X$ final $T)))$
$\equiv$ interchanging universal quantification with independent ranges
   $(\forall X : X \in V : (\forall p : p$ is a block :
   $(\forall T : T$ is a proper maximal computation of $\{ ||\, p,b \} : X$ final $T)))$
$\equiv$ because of the definition of final
   $(\forall X : X \in V : b \star X)$

From theorem 3, with V equal to the empty set, it follows that

$$(b \star \text{true}) \equiv \text{true}$$

and with V equal to the set $\{X,Y\}$,

$$(b \star (X \wedge Y)) \equiv ((b \star X) \wedge (b \star Y))$$

Theorem 4: Let c be a block such that all maximal computations of $\{|| \; c,b \; \}$ are proper. Then

$$(b \star B) \Rightarrow (\{|| \; c,b \; \} \star B)$$

Proof:

$b \star B$

$\equiv$ from definition of $\star$

    $(\forall p : p \text{ is a block} :$

    $(\forall T : T \text{ is a proper maximal computation of } \{|| \; p,b\} : B \text{ final } T))$

$\Rightarrow$ substitute $\{|| \; q,c\}$ for p, and use $\{|| \; \{|| \; q,c\},b\} = \{|| \; q, \{|| \; c, b\}\}$

    $(\forall q : q \text{ is a block} :$

    $(\forall T : T \text{ is a proper maximal computation of } \{|| \; q, \{|| \; c, b\}\} : B \text{ final } T))$

$\Rightarrow$ from definition of $\star$

    $\{|| \; c, b\} \star B.$

Theorem 5: For any finite set K,

$$(\forall i : i \in K : b_i \star B_i) \Rightarrow \{|| \; i : i \in K : b_i\} \star (\forall i : i \in K : B_i)$$

Proof:

$(\forall i : i \in K : b_i \star B_i)$

$\Rightarrow$ from theorem 4,

    $(\forall i : i \in K : \{|| \; j : j \in K : b_j\} \star B_i)$

$\Rightarrow$ from theorem 3,

    $\{|| \; i : i \in K : b_i\} \star (\forall i : i \in K : B_i)$

Theorem 6: $(x = e) \star (x \stackrel{\text{def}}{=} e)$

Proof: In any proper maximal computation of $\{|| \; x{=}e, \; p\}$, for any block p, from fairness eventually the definition statement $x{=}e$ is executed, and in all succeeding states $x \stackrel{\text{def}}{=} e$ holds.

Theorem 7: For any finite set K,

$$(\forall i : i \in K : b_i \star B_i)$$

$$\Rightarrow$$

$$(\{ ? i : i \in K : g_i -> b_i \} \star ((\exists i : i \in K : g_i \sim \text{true})$$

$$\equiv$$

$$(\exists i : i \in K : (g_i \sim \text{true}) \wedge B_i)))$$

Proof: Let us call the choice block b. In any proper maximal computation of $\{ || \ b,p \}$ for any block p, if $(\exists i : i \in K : g_i \sim \text{true})$ holds in any state in the computation, then at some later state block b_j that has a guard g_j where $g_j \sim$ true in that state, is initiated, and hence B_j holds in that state or a later state and continues to hold. Also, once g_j holds it continues to hold, because we restrict attention here to guards that do not reference mutable variables (but can reference definition variables). Hence, eventually, $g_j \wedge B_j$ holds and continues to hold.

Theorem 8: If at most one guard holds, then a choice composition block establishes the following conjunction of implications:

$$[(\forall i,j : g_i \wedge g_j : i = j)] \wedge (\forall i : i \in K : b_i \star B_i)$$

$$\Rightarrow$$

$$(\{ ? i : i \in K : g_i -> b_i \} \star (\forall i : i \in K : (g_i \sim \text{true}) \Rightarrow B_i)$$

Proof: Follows from Theorem 7 and the predicate calculus.

13.2.1   Specification Notation

We give both informal and formal specifications of programs in this chapter. For specifications, we use the notation of the predicate calculus with the following conventions:

1. We use both $\wedge$ and "," for *logical and*, where $\wedge$ has the usual binding power of the predicate calculus, and "," has lower binding power than any other operator except $\equiv$.

2. We use $\{ g_0 \ldots g_n \}$ to denote the quantification $(\forall i : 0 \leq i \leq n : g_i \sim \text{true})$. This is an overloading of the brace symbols, but this overloading should not cause confusion.

13.2.2   Dummy Variables

Local Variables in Parallel Blocks. Consider a block b in some program p. A variable that is **local** to b is a variable referenced within the text of b and which is not referenced elsewhere in the text of p. Let variable v be local to b. Then, the following proof rule is valid for handling local variables in blocks:

$$b(v) \star (\exists v :: B(v))$$

where the notation $b(v)$, $B(v)$ merely identifies that b and B reference v.

Dummy Variables in Pattern Matches. A pattern match $x ? = pat$ succeeds if and only if definition variable x reduces to a tuple of the same shape as pat, in which case dummy variables in the pattern become bound to corresponding elements of x. For example, the pattern match $x ? = \{hd, tl\}$ succeeds if and only if x is a two-tuple, in which case dummy variables hd and tl become bound to $x[0]$ and $x[1]$ respectively.

We postulate that

$$\{ ? i : i \in K : x_i ? = pat_i(u_i, v_i, \ldots), g_i(u_i, v_i, \ldots) \rightarrow b_i(u_i, v_i, \ldots) \} \star$$
$$(\exists i : i \in K : (\exists u_i, v_i, \ldots :: \{x_i = pat_i(u_i, v_i, \ldots)\}, \{g_i(u_i, v_i, \ldots)\})) \equiv$$
$$(\exists i : i \in K : (\exists u_i, v_i, \ldots :: \{x_i = pat_i(u_i, v_i, \ldots)\}, \{g_i(u_i, v_i, \ldots)\}, B_i(u_i, v_i, \ldots)))$$

where, for all i, $b_i(u_i, v_i, \ldots) \star B_i(u_i, v_i, \ldots)$.

Dummy variables in pattern matches are instantiated in this equation with existential quantification. Note, however, that there is *precisely one* value of the dummy variables u, v,...such that $x = pattern(u, v, \ldots)$. Therefore, if at most one guard holds, then (from the predicate calculus)

$$\{ ? i : i \in K : x_i ? = pat_i(u_i, v_i, \ldots), g_i(u_i, v_i, \ldots) \rightarrow b_i(u_i, v_i, \ldots) \} \star$$
$$(\forall i : i \in K : (\forall u_i, v_i, \ldots :: \{x_i = pat_i(u_i, v_i, \ldots)\}, \{g_i(u_i, v_i, \ldots)\} : B_i(u_i, v_i, \ldots)))$$

13.2.3   Recursion

We are required to design programs p such that $p \star P$. Predicate P may be defined by a recursive formula. In general, a recursive definition of P may admit an arbitrary number of solutions for P. In PCN we restrict attention to **weakest solutions** of recursive formulas. P is the weakest solution if and only if it is a solution and, for any other solution Q, $Q \Rightarrow P$.

In this book, if P is defined recursively, then the definition is monotonic in P and hence has a weakest solution. A complete discussion of extreme solutions of recursive equations is inappropriate for this book.

Consider a predicate $CLOCK(x)$ defined recursively as

$$[CLOCK(x) \equiv (\exists y :: x \stackrel{def}{=} [\text{``tick''} | y] \wedge CLOCK(y))]$$

This equation admits more than one solution for CLOCK. One solution (the so-called "strongest" solution) is CLOCK(x) ≡ false, for all x. The weakest solution is that CLOCK(x) holds if and only if x is an infinitely long sequence of "tick".

Consider a program that generates an infinite sequence of "tick"

$$clock(x) \{|| x = [\text{"tick"} | y], clock(y)\}$$

There is no **finite** computation of clock(x) after which CLOCK(x) holds because there is no finite computation that defines x to be an **infinite** number of "tick". We can prove, however, that the elements of x defined in a finite computation of clock(x) are equal to the corresponding elements of an x that satisfies CLOCK(x), and as the computation progresses, the number of the elements defined gets larger, and the limiting value of the predicate established by clock(x), as its computation tends to infinity, is CLOCK(x). Therefore, we must extend the notion of "establishes" to include limiting values as lengths of computations tend to infinity. For the remainder of this book, however, we only consider recursive definitions with finite depth.

13.3 Summary of Proof Rules

Hereafter we use lower-case letters for program names and upper-case letters for predicates; we shall use the same names for programs and the predicates they establish: thus b ⋆ B.

1. $(x = e) \star (x \stackrel{\text{def}}{=} e)$
2. $\{|| i : i \in K : b_i \} \star (\forall i : i \in K : B_i)$
3. $\{ ? i : i \in K : g_i \rightarrow b_i \} \star$
   $((\exists i : i \in K : g_i \sim \text{true}) \equiv (\exists i : i \in K : (g_i \sim \text{true}) \wedge B_i))$
4. If at most one guard holds:
   $\{ ? i : i \in K : g_i \rightarrow b_i \} \star (\forall i : i \in K : (g_i \sim \text{true}) \Rightarrow B_i)$

13.4 Examples

Next, we develop a few simple programs. Our goal here is to show that specifications can be transformed into programs in a simple, almost mechanical manner.

13.4.1 Split a List into Two

Develop a program split(x,left,right) where all arguments are definition variables, x is a finite input list, and left and right are output lists. List left contains some of the elements of x, and right contains the remaining elements of x. The lengths of left and right differ by at most 1, so left and right each contain about half the elements of x.

Specifications. We refine the given specification to the following convenient form.

1. If x reduces to the empty list, then left is defined as [ ] and right is defined as [ ].

2. If x reduces to a singleton list – i.e., a list containing precisely one element – then left is defined as x and right is defined as [ ].

3. If x contains two or more elements, let the head of x be dummy variable u, and let the next element in x be dummy variable v, and let the list that follows be dummy variable y; then define l and r by split(y,l,r), and define left as [u | l] and define right as [v | r].

Formal Specification. Develop a program split(x,left,right) where split(x,left,right) $\star$ SPLIT(x,left,right) and the SPLIT predicate is as shown in Specification 13.1.

$\text{SPLIT}(x, \text{left}, \text{right}) \equiv$

$((x = [\,]) \sim \text{true} \Rightarrow (\text{left} \stackrel{\text{def}}{=} [\,]) \wedge (\text{right} \stackrel{\text{def}}{=} [\,]))$

$\wedge$

$(\forall u :: (x = [u]) \sim \text{true} \Rightarrow ((\text{left} \stackrel{\text{def}}{=} x) \wedge (\text{right} \stackrel{\text{def}}{=} [\,])))$

$\wedge$

$(\forall u,v,y :: (x = [u,v \,|\, y]) \sim \text{true} \Rightarrow$

$(\text{SPLIT}(y,l,r) \wedge (\text{left} \stackrel{\text{def}}{=} [u \,|\, l]) \wedge (\text{right} \stackrel{\text{def}}{=} [v \,|\, r])))$

Specification 13.1 SPLIT(x,left,right)

Program. Program 13.1 is derived from the specification.

13.4.2 Merge Two Lists into One

Develop a program join(left,right,x) where all arguments are definition variables, x is an output list, and left and right are finite input lists of numbers, in nondecreasing order. Variable x contains all elements of left and right, and is in nondecreasing order.

Program Specification. We cast the specification in a convenient form. As an example, we shall employ a nondeterministic specification. The program establishes:

```
split(x,left,right)
{ ? x ? = [ ]      -> {|| left = [ ], right = [ ]},
    x ? = [u]      -> {|| left = x, right = [ ]},
    x ? = [u,v | y]  -> {|| split(y,l,r), left = [u | l], right = [v | r] }
}
```

Program 13.1 split(x,left,right)

if

1. left reduces to the empty list, or
2. right reduces to the empty list, or
3. both left and right reduce to nonempty lists,

then

1. left reduces to the empty list, and x is defined as right (because join of the empty list and right is right), or
2. right reduces to the empty list, and x is defined as left, or
3. both left and right reduce to nonempty lists, and q holds, where q is defined later.

Formal Specification. Develop a program join(left,right,x) where join(left,right,x) ⋆ JOIN(left,right,x) and the JOIN predicate is as shown in Specification 13.2.

$$
\begin{aligned}
&\text{JOIN(left,right,x)} \equiv \\
&(\text{left} = [\,]) \sim \text{true} \ \lor \\
&(\text{right} = [\,]) \sim \text{true} \ \lor \\
&(\exists u,v,l,r :: ((\text{left} = [u \mid l]) \sim \text{true}) \land ((\text{right} = [v \mid r]) \sim \text{true})) \\
&\Rightarrow \\
&(((\text{left} = [\,]) \sim \text{true}) \land x \stackrel{\text{def}}{=} \text{right}) \ \lor \\
&(((\text{right} = [\,]) \sim \text{true}) \land x \stackrel{\text{def}}{=} \text{left}) \ \lor \\
&(\exists u,v,l,r :: ((\text{left} = [u \mid l]) \sim \text{true}) \land ((\text{right} = [v \mid r]) \sim \text{true}) \land Q)
\end{aligned}
$$

Specification 13.2 JOIN(left,right,x)

Program. The program stub corresponding to this specification is shown in Program 13.2.

```
join(left,right,x)
{ ?   left ? = []                          -> x = right,
      right ? = []                         -> x = left,
      left ? = [u | l], right ? = [v | r]  -> q
}
```

Program 13.2 join(left,right,x)

Specifications of q.

1. If $u \leq v$, then x is defined as [u | y] and y is defined in join(l,right,y).

2. If $u > v$, then x = [v | y] and y is defined in join(left,r,y).

Formal Specification of q. Develop a program q where: q $\star$ Q and the Q predicate is as shown in Specification 13.3.

$$Q \equiv$$
$$((u \leq v) \sim true) \Rightarrow ((x \stackrel{def}{=} [u | y]) \wedge join(l,right,y))$$
$$\wedge$$
$$((u > v) \sim true) \Rightarrow ((x \stackrel{def}{=} [v | y]) \wedge join(left,r,y))$$

Specification 13.3 Q

Program. The program derived from the specification for stub q is shown in Program 13.3.

```
{ ?  u ≤ v   ->   {|| x = [u | y], join(l,right,y) },
     u > v   ->   {|| x = [v | y], join(left,r,y) }
}
```

Program 13.3 q

Putting the stubs together gives us the complete program:

```
join(left,right,x)
{ ? left ? = []                              -> x = right,
     right ? = []                            -> x = left,
     left ? = [u | l], right ? = [v | r]     ->
          { ? u ≤ v -> {|| x = [u | y], join(l,right,y) },
               u > v -> {|| x = [v | y], join(left,r,y) }
          }

}
```

13.4.3   Height of a Binary Tree

Develop a program ht(t,z), where t is a finite input binary tree and z is an output variable defined as the height of the tree. A tree t is either the empty tuple, { }, or a 3-tuple {left, val, right }, where left and right are the left and right subtrees of t, respectively, and val is the value associated with the root node. Both t and z are definition variables.

Specifications.

1. If t reduces to the empty tree, { } , then z is defined as 0.

2. If t reduces to a nonempty tree, let left, val, and right be the components t[0], t[1], and t[2] of tuple t; let ht_l be defined by ht(left, ht_l), let ht_r be defined by ht(right, ht_r), and let z be defined as follows.

   If ht_l ≥ ht_r then z = 1+ ht_l, and if ht_l < ht_r then z = 1 + ht_r.

Formal Specification.   Develop a program ht(t,z) where ht(t,z) ⋆ HT(t,z) and the HT specification is as shown in Specification 13.4.

Program.   The program developed from Specification 13.4 is shown in Program 13.4.

13.4.4   Quicksort with Copying

In this section we present C.A.R. Hoare's quicksort program, q, that uses definitions.

Program q(x,b,e) has input definition variables x and b and output definition variable e. Program q is required to define e as the nondecreasing-order sort of finite list x concatenated with b. For example, if b = [5, 4] and x = [2, 3, 1], then e = [1, 2, 3, 5, 4].

$HT(t,z) \equiv$

$((t = \{ \}) \sim true) \Rightarrow (z \overset{def}{=} 0)$

$\land$

$(\forall\, left, val, right :: ((t = \{left,val,right\}) \sim true) \Rightarrow$
$(\exists\, ht\_l, ht\_r :: HT(left, ht\_l) \land HT(right, ht\_r) \land$

$(((ht\_l \geq ht\_r) \sim true) \Rightarrow z \overset{def}{=} 1 + ht\_l)$

$\land$

$(((ht\_l < ht\_r) \sim true) \Rightarrow z \overset{def}{=} 1 + ht\_r)))$

Specification 13.4 $HT(t,z)$

```
ht(t,z)
{ ? t ?= { }                      ->   z = 0,
        t ?= {left, val, right}   ->   {|| ht(left, ht_l), ht(right, ht_r),
             { ? ht_l >= ht_r     ->   z = 1 + ht_l,
                   ht_l < ht_r    ->   z = 1 + ht_r
             }
        }
}
```

Program 13.4 $ht(t,z)$

Specifications.

1. If x reduces to the empty list, then e is defined as b.
2. If x reduces to a nonempty list, let its head be called v, and let its tail be called xs; let left and right be defined by partition(v,xs,left,right), where partition is described later, and let r be defined by q0(right,b,r), and let e be defined by q(left,[v | r],e).

Program partition(v,xs,left,right) defines left to be all elements of xs that are at most v, and defines right to be all elements of xs that exceed v.

Formal Specification. Develop a program q(x,b,e) where

$$q(x,b,e) \star Q(x,b,e)$$

where Q is as shown in Specification 13.5.

Program. The program derived from the specification is shown in Program 13.5.

$Q(x,b,e) \equiv$
$(((x = [\,]) \sim \text{true}) \Rightarrow (e \overset{\text{def}}{=} b))$
$\land$
$(\forall v, xs :: ((x = [v \mid xs]) \sim \text{true}) \Rightarrow$
$(\exists \text{left},\text{right},r :: \text{PARTITION}(v,xs,\text{left},\text{right}) \land Q(\text{right},b,r) \land Q(\text{left},[v \mid r],e)))$

Specification 13.5 $Q(x,b,e)$

$q(x,b,e)$
$\{ ? \ x ? = [\,] \qquad \rightarrow e = b,$
$\quad x ? = [v \mid xs] \qquad \rightarrow$
$\qquad\qquad \{\mid\mid \text{partition}(v,xs,\text{left},\text{right}), q(\text{right},b,r), q(\text{left},[v \mid r],e) \}$
$\}$

Program 13.5 $q(x,b,e)$

Specification of partition(v,xs,left,right).

1. If xs reduces to the empty list, then left is defined as [ ], and right is defined as [ ].

2. If xs reduces to a nonempty list, let us call its head and tail h and t respectively;

   (a) If $h \leq v$, then left = [h|ls], ls and right are defined by partition(v,t,ls,right).

   (b) If $h > v$, then right = [h|rs], rs and left are defined by partition(v,t,left,rs).

Formal Specification. Develop a program partition(v,xs,left,right) where partition(v,xs,left,right) $\star$ PARTITION(v,xs,left,right) and PARTITION is defined in Specification 13.6.

Program. The program derived from the specification is shown in Program 13.6.

13.4.5 Nondeterministic Merge of Finite Lists

Program mrg(x,y,z) has finite input lists x and y, and output list z. The output z is an interleaving of x and y, i.e., the elements of z are the elements of x and y, and the order of elements in x and in y are preserved in z.

Example. For x = [4, 12, 20], y = [3, 15, 7], some example values of z are z = [4, 12, 3, 15, 7, 20], z = [4, 3, 15, 7, 12, 20], and z = [3, 15, 4, 7, 12, 20]. The

PARTITION(v,xs,left,right) ≡

$(((xs = [\,]) \sim true) \Rightarrow (left \overset{def}{=} [\,]) \wedge (right \overset{def}{=} [\,]))$

$\wedge$

$(\forall h,t :: ((xs = [h\,|\,t]) \sim true) \Rightarrow$

$\qquad ((h \leq v) \Rightarrow (\exists ls :: (left \overset{def}{=} [h\,|\,ls]) \wedge PARTITION(v,t,ls,right)) \wedge$

$\qquad ((h > v) \Rightarrow (\exists rs :: (right \overset{def}{=} [h\,|\,rs]) \wedge PARTITION(v,t,left,rs))$

$\qquad)$

$)$

Specification 13.6 Q(x,b,e)

```
partition(v,xs,left,right)
{ ? xs ? = [ ]      -> {| | left = [ ], right = [ ]},
    xs ? = [h | t]  -> { ? h ≤ v -> {| | left = [h | ls], partition(v,t,ls,right) },
                             h > v -> {| | right = [h | rs], partition(v,t,left,rs) }
      }
}
```

Program 13.6 partition(v,xs,left,right)

following cannot be values of z: [4, 3, 15, 7, 20, 12] because 20 appears before 12, [4, 3, 15, 7, 12] because 20 does not appear, and [4, 3, 15, 7, 12, 20, 19] because 19 appears in z but not in x or y.

The output is not a function of the inputs, i.e., for given inputs there can be more than one output that satisfies the predicate.

Specifications. Program mrg establishes MRG(x,y,z) defined as follows. If x reduces to a list or y reduces to a list, then

1. x reduces to the empty list and z = y, or

2. x reduces to a nonempty list, and calling the head and tail of x, hx and tx respectively, z = [hx|zs], where zs satisfies MRG(tx,y,zs), or, by symmetry,

3. y reduces to the empty list and z = x, or

4. y reduces to a nonempty list, and calling the head and tail of y, hy and ty respectively, z = [hy | zs], where zs satisfies MRG(x,ty,zs).

The reason for case 1 is obvious: If z is an interleaving of an empty list and y then z is y. The reason for case 2 is that if x is nonempty, then we can define z as [hx|zs] where zs is defined to satisfy MRG(tx,y,zs), where hx and tx are the head and tail of x, respectively. This is because we can define z as the head of x plus a mrg of the remainder of x and all of y. Note that this is not the only way to define z, but it is one of the acceptable ways of doing so. The reasons for cases 3 and 4 follow by symmetry.

The proof that this specification is indeed a refinement of the one given earlier is by induction on the pair of natural numbers (lx,ly) which are the lengths of lists x and y, respectively. Note that the depth of recursion is finite because the lengths of the input lists are finite.

Formal Specification. Develop a program mrg(x,y,z) where

$$mrg(x,y,z) \star MRG(x,y,z)$$

and the MRG(x,y,z) predicate is as shown in Specification 13.7.

MRG(x,y,z) ≡
((x = [ ]) ~ true)
∨
(∃ hx,tx :: (x = [hx | tx]) ~ true)
∨
((y = [ ]) ~ true)
∨
(∃ hy,ty :: (y = [hy | ty]) ~ true)
≡
(((x = [ ]) ~ true) ∧ (z $\overset{\text{def}}{=}$ y))
∨
(∃ hx,tx :: ((x = [hx | tx]) ~ true) ∧ (z $\overset{\text{def}}{=}$ [hx | zs]) ∧ MRG(tx,y,zs))
∨
(((y = [ ]) ~ true) ∧ (z $\overset{\text{def}}{=}$ x))
∨
(∃ hy,ty :: ((y = [hy | ty]) ~ true) ∧ (z $\overset{\text{def}}{=}$ [hy | zs]) ∧ MRG(x,ty,zs))

Specification 13.7 MRG(x,y,z)

Program. The program derived from the formal specification is shown in Program 13.7.

```
mrg(x,y,z)
{ ? x = []            -> z = y,
    x ?= [hx | tx]    -> {|| z = [hx | zs], mrg(tx,y,zs)},
    y = []            -> z = x,
    y ?= [hy | ty]    -> {|| z = [hy | zs], mrg(x,ty,zs)}
}
```

Program 13.7 mrg(x,y,z)

13.5 Termination

Before we discuss sequential composition, we discuss termination of parallel and choice blocks and definition statements. From the operational semantic we have the following conditions.

Definition Statements: Execution of a definition statement always terminates.

Parallel Composition: A parallel block terminates execution if all its constituent blocks terminate execution.

Choice Composition: A choice block terminates execution if all its guards reduce to false or at least one of its guards reduces to true and for all its guards that reduce to true the corresponding blocks terminate execution.

We introduce a predicate $T.b$ with the following meaning: Block b terminates execution in any execution of a parallel block $\{|| p,b\}$, for any block p for which all maximal computations of the parallel block are proper, if

$$\{|| p,b\} \star T.b$$

We define $T.b$ as follows:

Definition Statement: $[T.(x=e) \equiv true]$

Parallel Composition: Let c be the block $\{|| i : i \in J : b_i\}$.
Then: $[T.c \equiv (\forall i : i \in J : T.b_i)]$

Choice Composition: Let c be the block
$\{? i : i \in J : g_i -> b_i\}$. Then:
$[T.c \equiv$
$(\forall i : i \in J : g_i \sim false) \vee$
$((\exists i : i \in J : g_i \sim true) \wedge (\forall i : (i \in J) \wedge (g_i \sim true): T.b_i))]$

13.6 Introduction of Mutables and Sequencing

If a program that uses only parallel and choice composition and definition variables does not have adequate efficiency, we introduce mutables and sequential composition into the most inefficient parts of the program. Alternatively, if we already have programs in C, Fortran or another language, we use them directly.

We use the following steps in the introduction of mutables and sequencing into a parallel block.

1. We order the statements in the parallel block so that all variables that appear on the right-hand sides of definition statements reduce to ground values or tuples, and all guards reduce to the ground values true or false, given only the definitions established by statements earlier in the ordering. In other words, we order statements in the direction of data flow; statements that write a variable appear earlier than statements that read that variable. Then we convert the parallel block into a sequential block by replacing "||" by ";" retaining the data-flow order of statements.

2. Next, we introduce mutables, add assignment statements to our program, and show that a mutable m has the same value as the definition variable x it is to replace, at every point in the program in which x is read – i.e., where x appears on the right-hand side of a definition statement or assignment or in a guard.

3. Finally, we remove the definition variables that are replaced by mutables, secure in the knowledge that the mutables have the same value as the definition variables in the statements in which they are read. We must, of course, be sure that mutables shared by constituent blocks of a parallel block are not modified within the parallel block.

Next, we develop a few simple programs using mutables.

13.6.1 Accumulator with Mutables

For convenience, we describe problem accumulate again. Develop a program accumulate(x,b,e) with inputs list x and number b, and output number e, where all parameters are definition variables. The program is to define e as b plus the sum of all elements in x. The program we developed earlier is shown again in Program 13.8.

Assume that all elements of list x reduce to numbers. Then the results of partial sums, in the previous program, can be accumulated in a mutable variable. Let us attempt to replace definition variables b, e, and w by a single mutable variable m. Figure 13.1 shows the data flow in the program.

accumulate(x,b,e)
{ ? x ?= []   ->   e = b,
    x ?= [v | xs]   ->   {|| w = b+v, accumulate(xs,w,e)}
}

Program 13.8 accumulate(x,b,e)

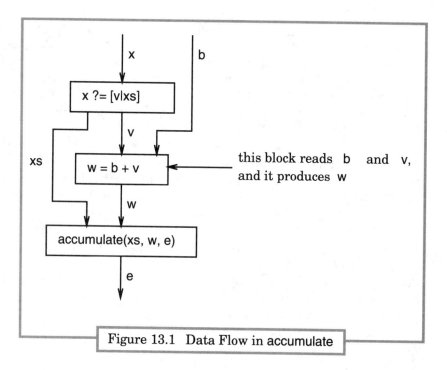

Figure 13.1   Data Flow in accumulate

The matching operation reads x and produces v and xs; the program call accumulate(xs,w,e) reads xs and w and produces e; the definition statement w = b + v reads b and v and produces w. A sequence consistent with the data flow is to carry out the pattern match first, then the definition statement, and finally call accumulate(xs,w,e), as in Program 13.9.

Having obtained a sequence consistent with the data flow, we introduce mutable variable m, into our program, to replace b, e and w; therefore, the value of m must equal the value of the variables that it is replacing, at the points that the replaced variables are used. We begin by developing a program that includes b, e, w, and m. Later, we shall remove b, e, and w.

```
accumulate(x,b,e)
{ ? x ?= []          -> e = b,
    x ?= [v | xs]     -> { ; w = b + v, accumulate(xs,w,e)}
}
```

Program 13.9 accumulate(x,b,e)

Assume that we are given initially that m = b. Variable b is used in two places: the definition statements e = b and w = b + v; we must be sure that the value of m at the point at which these statements are executed is equal to b. Likewise, we must be sure that m = w at points in the program where w is used, and that, at termination, m = e. Program 13.10 shows how m is modified so that it equals b, e and w at points at which they are used. We prove that definition variables in the right-hand sides of assignments and in guards reduce to ground values given only statements earlier in the ordering. Comments and assertions are between /* and */.

```
accumulate1(x,b,e,m)
int m;
/* m = b, by assumption */
{ ? x ?= []          -> e = b /* m = e */,
    x ?= [v | xs]     -> { ; /* m = b */
                            w = b + v,
                            m := m + v,
                            /* m = w */
                            accumulate1(xs,w,e,m)
                            /* by induction, m = e */
                         }
    /* m = e */
}
```

Program 13.10 accumulate1(x,b,e,m)

Next, we eliminate definition variables b, e, and w, using mutable variable m in their place (because we can assert that m is equal to b, e, and w at the points at which they are used) to get the program shown in Program 13.11.

The first guarded block, corresponding to the guard "x is empty", need not be included because in this case m and all other variables remain unchanged.

```
accumulate2(x,m)
int m;
{ ? x ?= [v | xs] -> { ; m : = m + v, accumulate2(xs,m) }
}
```

Program 13.11 accumulate2(x,m)

Let b be the initial value of m, and let e be the final value of m. Then e is b plus the sum of the elements in x.

Problem. Can we replace sequential composition in the last example by parallel composition?

13.6.2   Sum Function of Elements in a List

This example is to make you think about the relative efficiencies of sequential and parallel execution.

Specification. Let x be a list of numbers, and let x_i be the i-th element of list x, for $i \geq 0$. Let f(v,w) be a program with input v and output w, where both v and w are definition variables. We specify a program total(x,b,e) with input list x, input definition variable b, and output definition variable e, which defines e so that

$$e = b + \Sigma_i \; w_i$$

where w_i is defined by $f(x_i, w_i)$. For example, if f(x,w) sets $w = x^2$, then

$$e = b + \Sigma_i \; x_i^2$$

Refined Specification. We manipulate the specification into a convenient form.

1. If x reduces to the empty list then e is defined as b.
2. If x reduces to a nonempty list, call its head element v and its tail xs; define e as total(xs,y,e), and define y as b+w, and define w as f(v,w).

The formal specification is left to the reader.

Program. The refined specification suggests Program 13.12.

Introduction of Mutables. Next, we introduce mutables, using exactly the same steps as in sum, to get Program 13.13, where if b is the initial value

```
        total(x,b,e)
        { ? x ?= []          -> e = b,
              x ?= [v | xs]   -> {| | f(v,w), y = b+w, total(xs,y,e) }
        }
```

Program 13.12 total(x,b,e)

```
        total1(x,m)
        int m;
        { ? x ?= [v | xs]     ->  { ; f(v,w), m := m + w, total1(xs,m) }
        }
```

Program 13.13 total(x,m)

of m, and e is the final value of m, then the specification given earlier for total applies to total1 as well.

Efficiency. Which of the two programs, total or total1, is more efficient? Program total uses more memory than total1, but it offers more potential for parallel execution because it spawns programs f(v,w), for each element v of list x, in parallel. (In the interests of brevity we have not specified the locations at which processes are spawned.) Thus if f takes a long time to execute, x is a large list, and there are a large number of processors, then the parallel version can execute faster than the sequential version. Furthermore, if x is a list whose elements do not reduce to numbers until after total(x,b,e) terminates, then replacing total(x,b,e) by total1(x,m) results in a deadlock: Program total1 will not terminate because it will wait forever for an element of x to reduce to a ground value.

13.7 Summary

We can derive transformational parallel programs in PCN by manipulating a specification in the predicate calculus into a canonical form, and then mechanically translating the canonical form into a PCN program that does not use mutable variables or sequential composition. Later, mutable variables and sequential composition are introduced in a systematic manner that guarantees that the transformed program also satisfies the specification. Mutable variables are introduced to improve the efficiency of the program with regard to memory and time. PCN programs can be derived in a systematic manner, where most of the work of program derivation is that of deriving structured specifications from the given specification — and this work is carried out in the domain of specifications rather than in the domain of programming languages.

We have not used functions in this book to emphasize that calculations can be carried out in the predicate calculus without the use of functions and without too much added work. Of course, the introduction of functions simplifies the calculational effort in program derivation.

An alternative way of reasoning about parallel programs is to reason about the operations of all the processes. This operational way of developing programs can be difficult, because it can be hard to keep track of the operations of many different processes, especially when processes and communication channels are being instantiated and terminated. In particular, debugging this way can be quite difficult because most debugging tools do not keep track of dynamic creation and destruction of processes, nor do they keep global snapshots of what all processes are doing at any given time. We believe that the method of program development suggested in this chapter can be simpler than operational methods because it **directs your effort towards the specific goal of showing that a complex specification is a composition of simpler specifications** — this frees you from having to keep track of operations of lots of processes.

Exercises

1. Specify and then derive the merge sort program formally. Use the merge and split programs given in this chapter.

2. Specify and then derive a program to compute all prime numbers less than N, for some integer N, where $N > 2$. Use the Sieve of Eratosthenes.

3. Specify and derive a program to carry out a depth-first search in a directed graph. You are given a list of vertices, and for each vertex you are given a list of successors.

4. Use a tree-search algorithm, such as branch-and-bound, to solve the 0-1 Knapsack problem. The problem is as follows. Given N objects, where each object is specified by a weight and a value, and given a knapsack specified by some capacity C, determine the set of objects to be placed in the knapsack to maximize the value of the contents of the knapsack, subject to the constraint that the capacity of the knapsack not be exceeded.

5. Derive a program to solve the all-points, shortest-path problem in parallel.

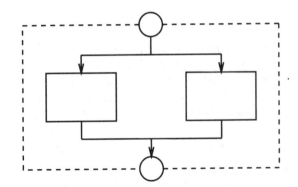

CHAPTER

14

Reactive Systems

> **Goals for this Chapter:**
>
> This chapter gives you a brief introduction to reactive systems. You will learn how to specify and reason about reactive systems.

A transformational program is specified by the predicates that hold in the initial and final states of the program. A reactive program is specified by properties of all computations of the program, including, perhaps, properties of states of the program other than its initial and final states.

14.1 Reactive System Examples

Your bank account is a simple reactive system. A specification of your bank account that specifies its states only when you open and close the account is incomplete. For instance, you may want to specify that in all states of all computations of the system, the amount in your account is the amount you put in minus the amount you took out (ignoring interest and service charges).

An **invariant** of a program is a predicate that holds in all states of all computations of the program. An invariant of your bank account is that the amount in it is the total amount put into it minus the total amount taken out of it.

You may also want to specify that if you present the bank with a withdrawal slip for x dollars, where x does not exceed the amount in your account, then the bank will give you x dollars. Since, our specification notation does not have clocks or time, we cannot say that the bank will give you the money in, say, two minutes, but we can say the bank will give you the money. In other words, we can specify that in all computations of the bank account, if a withdrawal slip for x dollars, where x does not exceed the amount in your account, is presented to the bank, then there is a later point in the execution at which the bank gives you x dollars.

Facts about states or state transitions that hold "eventually" are referred to as **progress properties** of the system, and facts that hold for all states or all bounded-length sequences of transitions are called **safety** properties. We can verify that finite computations satisfy, or do not satisfy, safety properties. We cannot, in general, demonstrate that a *finite* computation does not satisfy a progress property; this is because some state or transition may not have occurred in the finite computation, but can occur in extensions of the computation.

A great deal has been written about proving invariants and other safety properties. Here, we merely observe that a predicate X is an invariant of the parallel block {|| b_0, ..., b_n } if X is an invariant of all blocks b_i, for all i.

14.1.1 Example: Warning Lights on Parts

Consider the following system: A warning light turns on after a part fails and remains on thereafter. The warning light is off until the part fails.

An invariant of the system is: If the warning light is on, then the part has failed. In other words, in any state of any execution, if the warning light is on, then the part has failed in that state. A progress property of the system is: If the part fails, then the warning light *will* come on. Note that it is possible for the part to have failed and for the warning light not to have come on yet. The specification only says that after the part fails, the warning light will come on eventually.

Let X and Y be boolean definition variables, where X is defined if and only if the part has failed, and Y is defined if and only if the light is on. Let defined.Z, where Z is a definition variable, be a predicate that holds if and only if Z is defined. Thus,

$$[\text{defined.}z \equiv \neg\, \mathcal{U}.z]$$

An invariant of our system is: If Y is defined, then X is defined.

Invariant. defined.Y $\Rightarrow$ defined.X

Progress properties are specified by using the "establishes" operator. Our system establishes that if the part has failed then the warning light is on. This is because in all computations of our system and its environment, if the part has failed then *eventually* the warning light is on. Let us call the system consisting of the part and its warning light b. Our progress property is that b establishes that if X is defined then Y is also defined.

Progress. b ⋆ (defined.X ⇒ defined.Y)

14.1.2   Example: Specification of Copy

We specify a program copy(in,out), where in is an input list and out is an output list, and where the program copies its input to its output as follows:

Invariant of copy(in,out). If out is a sequence $v_0, \ldots, v_k$ followed by x, then there is some y such that in is the same sequence, $v_0, \ldots, v_k$, followed by y. In other words, the sequence of elements that are in the output are also in the input.

Invariant. out = $[v_0, \ldots, v_k \mid x] \Rightarrow (\exists y :: in = [v_0, \ldots, v_k \mid y])$

Progress. The progress property specifies that the sequence of elements in the input eventually appear in the output. Thus, the program establishes that, if $v_0, \ldots, v_k$ is in the input, then it is eventually also in the output.

$$copy(in,out) \star (in = [v_0, \ldots, v_k \mid y] \Rightarrow (\exists x :: out = [v_0, \ldots, v_k \mid x]))$$

The program also establishes that if in is a finite list then out=in.

$$copy(in,out) \star (in = [v_0, \ldots, v_k] \quad \Rightarrow \quad out=in)$$

```
copy(in,out)
{ ? in ?= [m | more_in] ->
            {||  out = [m | more_out],
                copy(more_in,more_out)
            },
        in ?= [ ] -> out = in
}
```

Program 14.1 copy program

14.2 Fair Merge

Consider program mrg given in the previous chapter. Program mrg(left,right,z) copies elements from its input lists left and right into its output list z. An invariant of the program is: All elements in the output are elements of one of the inputs, and the order of elements in each of the inputs is preserved in the output. The program does not have the progress property that all elements of left and right are eventually copied into z. This is because if left is an infinite list, then the program can copy elements only from left and copy no elements from right.

We need a program such as fair_join(left,right,z) that has the invariant properties of mrg(left,right,z) and, in addition, has the progress property that all elements in inputs left and right eventually appear in the output z, even if left or right are infinite lists.

14.2.1 Operation of Merger

We shall use a program merger(y,z), provided by PCN which operates as follows. The input to the program is list y and its output is list z. The program copies elements of list y into list z except for elements that are 2-tuples of the form {"merge", x} for some list x. When a 2-tuple {"merge", x} is read, the program starts copying elements of x into z and it continues to copy elements of y into z; thus it interleaves copying of list x and the remainder of list y into z. When the program reads a 2-tuple {"merge", w} in any of its inputs, the program starts copying elements of list w into z as well as continuing to copy elements of its other input lists into z. Thus the program can merge an arbitrary number of lists into a single list. All elements of all input lists of merger other than commands of the form {"merge",w}, eventually appear in the output list. The order of elements in any input list is preserved in the output list: if u appears before v in an input list then u appears before v in the output list as well; also, if u appears before {"merge",w} in an input list and v appears in w then u appears before v in the output list.

14.2.2 Specification of Merger

We define a predicate appears(x,y) as follows: appears(x,y) holds if and only if y reduces to a list and there exists some k such that the k-th element of y reduces to x. Thus, appears(x,y) holds if and only if x appears in list y. We define a predicate generates(w,v) as follows: generates(w,v) holds if and only if v appears in w or w reduces to a list and there is a chain of lists w, a, b, c,...,h, where {"merge",a} is in list w, {"merge",b} is in list a, {"merge",c} is in list b,..., and v appears in list h. Thus, generates is the strongest solution of

[generates(w,v) =
     (appears(v,w) ∨ (∃ u : appears({"merge",u},w) : generates(u,v)))]

Assume that all the elements in all the input lists x, (i.e., for all x such that generates(y,x) holds) are unique; we can tag elements appropriately to distinguish them, if necessary, where the tags are employed only to simplify the specification.

> **Merger Invariant (I):** An invariant of the merger(y,z) is: All elements in the output list are elements in an input list, and the output does not contain elements of the form {"merge", v}.

Invariant. appears(x,z) ⇒ (generates(y,x) ∧ (x ≠ {"merge", v}))

> **Merger Progress:** A progress property is that all elements in input lists, other than tuples of the form {"merge", v}, eventually appear in the output.

Thus, merger(y,z) establishes that all elements x generated by y, other than elements of the form {"merge", v}, appear in z.

Progress. merger(y,z) ⋆ ((generates(y,x) ∧ (x ≠ {"merge", v})) ⇒ appears(x,z))

Define predicate order(u,v,x) as the strongest solution of:
- x reduces to a list, and u appears earlier than v in list x (i.e., there exists j and k, such that $j < k$ and the j-th element of x is defined to be u, and the k-th element of x is defined to be v), or
- there exists a w such that u appears earlier than {"merge", w} in x and generates(w,v), or
- there exists t such that generates(x,t) ∧ order(u,v,t).

> **Merger Invariant (II):** Another invariant property of merger is that the order of elements in an input list is preserved in the output.

Invariant. ¬ (order(u,v,y) ∧ order(v,u,z))

14.2.3 Example

We can define program fair_join(left,right,z) as merger([{"merge", right} | left],z), assuming that lists left and right do not, in turn, have elements of the form {"merge", v} for any v. We can also define the program as merger([{"merge", right}, {"merge", left}],z).

14.3 Examples of a Reactive System

In this section we develop a very simple example of a reactive system, a scheme for mutual exclusion. We begin by considering a simple token-passing scheme.

14.3.1 A Token Ring

Consider a parallel block (shown in Program 14.2) which is a composition of two copy processes, say one on the left and one on the right as shown in Figure 14.1. The output of each process is the input to the other, and the input to the left process has a token in it, initially, where the string "token" represents a token.

```
{|| copy(left_in,left_out),
    copy(right_in,right_out),
    right_in = left_out,
    left_in = ["token" | right_out]
}
```

Program 14.2 Token Ring

A process copy(in,out) receives a token by reading the string "token" in its input list, and it sends the token by writing the string on its output list. Define predicate $T^k(x)$ as: list x is a sequence of k instances of string "token" followed by an undefined value.

Safety Property. Given the invariant for copy discussed earlier in this chapter, we can show that there exists some k such that the token has appeared k times in right_out and it has appeared k or $k+1$ times in left_out. In other words, the token has made k cycles, starting at left_in and finishing at left_in, or it has completed k cycles, and is now in right_in on its $k+1$-th cycle.

Invariant. $(\exists k : T^k(\text{right\_out}) : T^k(\text{left\_out}) \lor T^{k+1}(\text{left\_out}))$

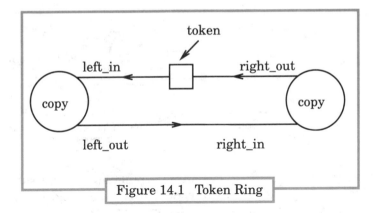

Figure 14.1   Token Ring

Progress Properties. Also, given the progress properties of copy we can show the following progress properties of the parallel block. If the token has appeared in left_out at least k times then the token will appear in right_out at least k times; also, if the token has appeared in right_out at least k times then the token will appear in left_out at least k+1 times; in other words, the block establishes

$$(R^k(\text{left\_out}) \Rightarrow R^k(\text{right\_out})) \;\wedge\; (R^k(\text{right\_out}) \Rightarrow R^{k+1}(\text{left\_out}))$$

where $R^k(x)$ is defined as: there exists a z such that list x is a sequence of k instances of string "token" followed by z. Therefore, the token circulates through the system infinitely often. The block establishes

$$(R^k(\text{left\_out}) \Rightarrow R^{k+1}(\text{left\_out})) \;\wedge\; (R^k(\text{right\_out}) \Rightarrow R^{k+1}(\text{right\_out}))$$

We now use the token-ring to design a mutual-exclusion program.

14.4 Mutual Exclusion

The mutual exclusion network consists of client and server programs, as shown in Figure 14.2. We consider an example with two clients and two servers. Each client and each server is called a process.

14.4.1 Client

Process client has an input list in, and an output lists out, a mutable boolean variable, cs, and perhaps other parameters that are not relevant here. The

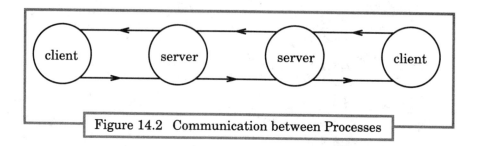

Figure 14.2   Communication between Processes

variable cs represents the critical section of the program — cs has value true if and only if the program is in a critical section. We wish to ensure that at most one client process is in a critical section in any state, i.e., at most one client process has a cs with value true. We do not care what the process does in its critical section; the only assumption we make is that the process remains in its critical section for finite time (i.e., a finite number of computational steps).

The process receives tokens along in and it sends tokens and requests for tokens along out. The process enters its critical section only if it holds a token. Initially, the process is not in its critical section, and it does not hold any tokens. When a process starts waiting to enter its critical section, it sends a request on out. When a waiting process receives a token on in, the process enters its critical section. The process sends the token on out when it leaves the critical section, as shown in Figure 14.3; the final program is shown in Program 14.2. We want to design a system in which the client receives a token within a finite number of steps of sending a request.

An invariant of the client is that the message (if any) following a request is a token.

Invariant. $(out^k = \text{"request"}) \wedge \text{defined.}out^{k+1} \Rightarrow (out^{k+1} = \text{"token"})$

where out^k is the k-th element of out.

14.4.2   Server

Mutual exclusion between clients is implemented by a network of servers. The network has one server for each client. A client communicates only with the server associated with it. A server communicates with its client and with other servers as shown in Figure 14.2. The server has input lists from_client and from_server, and output lists to_client and to_server. A server receives requests and tokens from its client. Servers send only tokens. The server merges both its input lists into a single list, z which feeds a process switch(z,to_client,to_server), as shown in Figure 14.4; the server program is shown in Program 14.3.

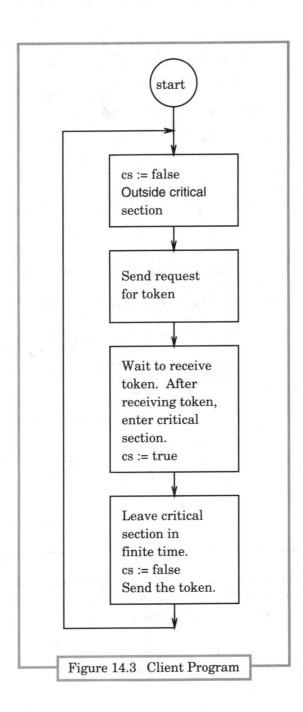

Figure 14.3 Client Program

```
client(in,out,cs)
int cs;
{ ;  /* The client is not in its critical section and cs = false
      * The client does not hold any tokens
      * The client spends arbitrary time outside its critical section
      * and then sends a request to enter its critical section
      */
   out = ["request" | more_out],
   /* The client waits to receive a token */
   { ? in ? = ["token" | more_in] ->
         /* The client has received a token. */
         /* The client can enter its critical section when it holds
         the token.
         */
            { ;  cs := true,
                 /* The client spends finite time in the critical section */
                 cs := false,
                 /* The client is now outside its critical section */
                 /* The client sends a token */
                 cs == false -> more_out = ["token" | next_out],
                 /* The client is not in its critical section and cs = false */
                 /* The client does not hold any tokens */
                 client(more_in,next_out,cs)
            }
   }
}
```

Program 14.3 Token Ring Program

```
server(from_client,from_server,to_client,to_server)
{|| fair_join(from_client,from_server,z),
    switch(z,to_client,to_server)
}
```

Program 14.4 Server

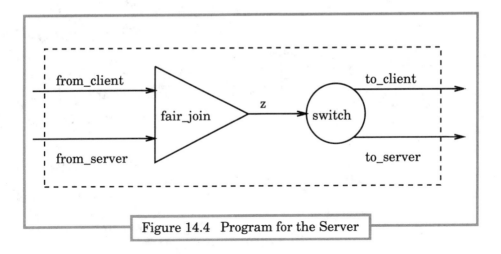

Figure 14.4 Program for the Server

14.4.3 Switch

Process switch(z,to_client,to_server) operates as follows. A token following a request in z is sent to the client, and a token that does not follow a request is sent to other servers, as shown in Figure 14.5.

```
switch(z,to_client,to_server)
{ ? z ? = ["token" | x]  ->
        {|| to_server = ["token" | more_to_server],
            switch(x,to_client,more_to_server)
        },
    z ? = ["request","token" | y]  ->
        {|| to_client = ["token" | more_to_client],
            switch(y,more_to_client,to_server)
        }
}
```

Program 14.5 Switch

14.4.4 Network

The network is shown in Figure 14.6. Initially, no client is in its critical section and there is a single token on the input to one of the servers. The program for the network is given in Program 14.6.

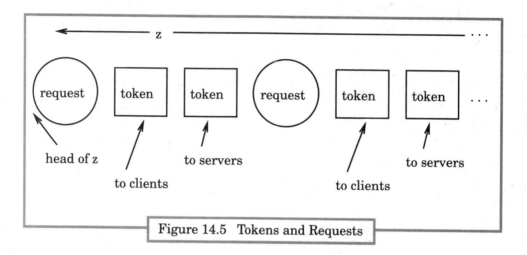

Figure 14.5   Tokens and Requests

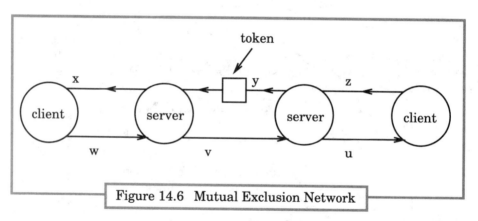

Figure 14.6   Mutual Exclusion Network

We leave it to the reader to prove that the program has invariants and progress properties similar to that of the token-passing system described earlier in this section. The parallel composition of a client and its server has the same invariant and progress properties as a copy process. In particular, an invariant is: There is precisely one token in the system. A progress property is that a client receives a token within a finite number of steps after sending a request.

14.5   Summary

This chapter gave you a very brief introduction to reactive systems. You saw examples of specifications of reactive systems using safety and progress prop-

```
            #define FALSE 0

            mutual_exclusion()
            int l,r;
            { ;  l := FALSE, r := FALSE,
               {||  client(x,w,l),
                    server(w,["token" | y], x,v),
                    client(u,z,r),
                    server(z,v,u,y)
               }
            }
```

Program 14.6 Mutual Exclusion

erties. A simple reactive program was developed, and the outline of its proof of correctness was given. You should now have some idea of how reactive systems can be designed in a compositional style.

Exercises

1. Write a program to find the first N prime numbers. Use the Sieve of Eratosthenes.

2. Specify and derive a program to solve the Distributed Dining Philosophers Problem. Given an arbitrary undirected graph, each vertex of the graph corresponds to a philosopher. A philosopher goes through cycles of the following three states: thinking, to hungry, to eating, to thinking. A thinking period is of arbitrary duration, and eating periods are of finite duration. The philosopher determines the transition form thinking to hungry, and from eating to thinking. Your program determines transitions from hungry to eating so that:

   (a) Neighboring philosophers are not eating at the same time. (Two philosophers are neighbors if there is an edge between them.)

   (b) A hungry philosopher eats eventually.

   Hint: Use a fork for each edge of the graph. A fork is shared by the two philosophers incident on the edge corresponding to the fork. A philosopher eats only when holding all forks for all incident edges. A fork becomes dirty when it is eaten with, and becomes clean when it is sent from one philosopher to another. A philosopher yields a dirty fork if it is requested, but does not yield a clean one.

3. Consider a special case of the previous problem in which the graph is completely connected. Since only one philosopher can eat at any one time, the problem is called the Mutual Exclusion Problem. Solve the problem as follows: A philosopher sends a request to the manager when hungry. Eventually, the manager replies to the request by sending the hungry philosopher a token. A hungry philosopher transits to eating upon receiving the token. When finished eating, the philosopher sends the token back to the manager, and transits to thinking. The system has precisely one token. Compare the efficiency of the solution to this problem to that of the previous problem.

4. Each process in a network of processes is either idle or active. An active process can send tasks to other processes. An idle process cannot send tasks to others. An idle process becomes active on receiving a task. An active process can become idle at any time. Initially, one process, say p, is active and all others are idle. Formally specify, and then develop, a program that determines when all processes are idle.

Further Reading

Here we provide a selective bibliography of material relevant to content of this book.

- G. Agha, "A Model of Concurrent Computation in Distributed Systems", MIT Press, Cambridge, Massachusetts, 1986.

  Gives a description of the semantic basis for Actor programs. Many PCN programs can be written as either actor or object-oriented programs.

- A.V. Aho, J.E. Hopcroft, and J.D. Ullman, "Data Structures and Algorithms", Addison-Wesley, Reading, Massachusetts, 1983.

  A comprehensive text on sequential algorithms. Several problems are considered, including searching and sorting, graph algorithms and matrix computation.

- D.P. Bertsekas and J.N. Tsitsiklis, "Parallel and Distributed Computation", Prentice-Hall, New Jersey, 1989.

  A detailed description of parallel algorithms for many problems in scientific computation and operations research.

- K.M. Chandy and J. Misra, "Parallel Program Design: A Foundation", Addison-Wesley, Reading, Massachusetts, 1988.

  A theory for nondeterministic programs is presented and the book shows how to develop programs using composition. The value of universal quantification in programs is demonstrated. Several programs are derived from specifications in a formal manner.

- E.W. Dijkstra and C. Scholten, "Predicate Calculus and Program Semantics", Springer-Verlag, New York, 1990.

  Presents the predicate calculus with applications to program semantics. PCN design methods and proof rules are based on the predicate calculus, this book provides a foundation on the subject.

- J.J. Dongarra, I.S. Duff, D.C. Sorensen, and H.A. Van der Vorst, "Solving Linear Systems on Vector and Shared Memory Computers", SIAM Publications, Philadelphia, Pennsylvania, 1991.

A description of basic linear algebra programs for parallel machines, with performance analysis and measurement on a variety of machines.

- I. Foster and S. Taylor, "Strand: New Concepts in Parallel Programming", Prentice-Hall, New Jersey, 1990.

  Describes early work on the practical use of *choice*, *interleaving* and *monotonicity*. Emphasizes methodical program construction by stepwise refinement and the decomposition of systems into modules.

- N. Francez, "Fairness", Springer-Verlag, New York, 1986.

  A comprehensive book on fairness.

- H. Glaser, C. Hankin, and D. Till, "Principles of Functional Programming", Prentice-Hall, New Jersey, 1984.

  An introduction to functional programming. Many PCN programs can be written as functional programs.

- S. Gregory, "Parallel Logic Programming in PARLOG", Addison-Wesley, Reading, Massachusetts, 1987.

  Describes early work in concurrent logic programming. Many PCN programs can be written as logic programs or using concurrent logic programming notations.

- D. Gries, "The Science of Programming", Springer-Verlag, New York, 1981.

  An introductory text on the systematic derivation of programs. Shows how proof rules help programmers to design programs. A large number of examples are presented.

- E.C.R. Hehner, "The Logic of Programming", Prentice-Hall, London, U.K., 1984.

  A theory of program correctness is presented. The way in which proof rules for assignment statements are given in Hehner's book is much the same as in our book. Hehner's idea that a program is a predicate is used in PCN.

- C.A.R. Hoare, "Communicating Sequential Processes", Prentice-Hall, London, U.K., 1984.

  A theory of communicating processes is presented. Hoare's theory, based on process traces, can be applied to PCN as well. Several reactive and transformational programs are presented with their correctness proofs.

- C.L. Seitz, "Multicomputers", in book "Developments in Concurrency and Communication", Editor C.A.R. Hoare, pp 131, Addison-Wesley, Reading, Massachusetts, 1991.

  A thorough discussion of the design of multicomputers, their low level programming systems and a number of interesting applications.

Appendix A. Predefined Programs

This appendix summarizes the guard tests and predefined programs used throughout this book.

A.1 Guard Tests

X == Y	X and Y are identical
X != Y	X and Y are not identical
X<Y	X is less than Y
X>Y	X is greater than Y
X <= Y	X is less than or equal to Y
X >= Y	X is greater than or equal to Y
int(X)	X is an integer
double(X)	X is a double precision floating point number
char(X)	X is a character string
tuple(X)	X is a tuple
data(X)	X is defined
X ?= Y	X matches pattern Y
default	all other guards are false

A.2 Predefined Programs

X=Y	define the definition variable X to be the value Y
X := Y	assign the mutable variable X to be the value Y
make_tuple(n,t)	builds a tuple t of size n
length(X)	the number of elements in X
merge(In,Out)	merge n-streams into stream Out via stream In
distribute(n,In)	distribute stream In to n output streams

Note that we implement lists using tuples of size two: A list [first | rest] is equivalent to {first,rest}. Similarly, the list [1,2,3,4] is equivalent to

$$\{1,\{2,\{3,\{4,\{5,\{\}\}\}\}\}\}$$

Thus both equivalence (==) and matching (?=) in these cases will succeed.

Appendix B. PCN Syntax

Non-terminal symbols begin with an uppercase letter; tokens are signified in uppercase and are identical to C. All other symbols are terminal symbols.

ModulePart	:: Form	ModulePart Form
Form	:: Heading Declarations Implication	-exports Args	-foreign Args
Heading	:: ID ( )	ID (NameList)
NameList	:: ID	NameList , ID
Declarations	:: empty	Declarations Declaration
Declaration	:: Type Mutables ;
Mutables	:: Mutable	Mutables , Mutable
Mutable	:: ID [ ]	Var
Implication	:: Block	Guard -> Block
Block	:: Var := Exp	Var = Value	ID	Call	{ Op Blocks }
Blocks	:: Implication	Blocks , Implication
Value	:: Exp	Tuple	List	STRING	Call
Op	::			?	;
Guard	:: Tests	default
Tests	:: Test	Tests , Test
Test	:: ID ? = Rhs	Con Eq Con	Exp Ar Exp	Type (Value)
Con	:: Exp	STRING	[ ]	{ }
Rhs	:: List	Tuple	Call
Eq	:: ==	!=
Ar	:: <	>	<=	>=
Type	:: int	double	char	tuple	data
Call	:: LocalCall	RemoteCall
LocalCall	:: QID : QID Args	QID Args
QID	:: ID	' ID
RemoteCall	:: LocalCall @ INTEGER	LocalCall @ QID
Args	:: ( )	(ArgList)
ArgList	:: Value	ArgList , Value
Exp	:: Term	Exp + Term	Exp – Term
Term	:: Factor	Term * Factor	Term Factor	Term % Factor
Factor	:: Num	(Exp)	length (ID)
Num	:: Numeric	– Numeric	Var
Numeric	:: INTEGER	REAL
Var	:: ID	ID [ID]	ID [INTEGER]
List	:: [ ]	[Elements]	[Elements	Element]
Tuple	:: { Elements }	{ }
Elements	:: Element	Elements , Element
Element	:: Num	STRING	List	Tuple	Call

Index

NOTES

NOTES

NOTES

NOTES

NOTES